SANDINISTAS SPEAK

SANDINISTAS SPEAK

by Tomás Borge, Carlos Fonseca, Daniel Ortega, Humberto Ortega, and Jaime Wheelock

Pathfinder Press

New York　　London　　Sydney

Fourth printing, 1986

Pathfinder Press
410 West Street, New York, New York 10014
Distributors:
Africa, Europe, and the Middle East:
  Pathfinder Press, 47 The Cut, London SE1 8LL England
Asia, Australia, and the Pacific:
  Pathfinder Press, P.O. Box 37, Leichhardt, Sydney, NSW 2040 Australia
Canada:
  DEC Book Distribution, 229 College St., Toronto, Ontario M5T 1R4 Canada
New Zealand:
  Pilot Books, Box 8730, Auckland, New Zealand

Contents

Introduction 7

The Historic Program of the FSLN 13

Nicaragua: Zero Hour
  By Carlos Fonseca Amador 23

Nothing Will Hold Back Our Struggle for Liberation
  By Daniel Ortega 43

Nicaragua — The Strategy of Victory
  Interview with Humberto Ortega 53

On Human Rights in Nicaragua
  By Tomás Borge 85

The Role of Religion in the New Nicaragua 105

Nicaragua's Economy and the Fight Against Imperialism
  By Jaime Wheelock 113

The Second Anniversary of the Sandinista Revolution
  By Tomás Borge 127

An Appeal for Justice and Peace
  By Daniel Ortega 141

Index 155

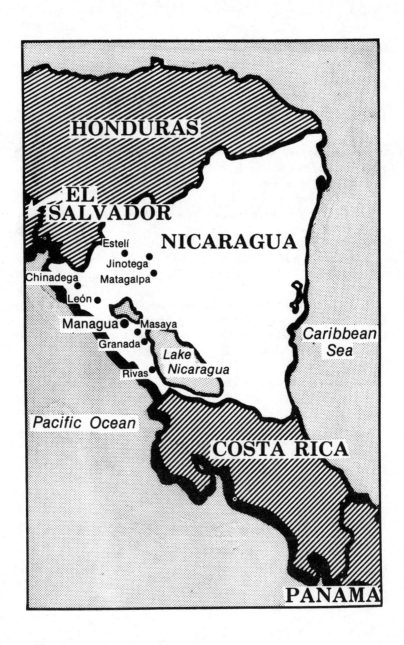

HONDURAS

EL
SALVADOR

NICARAGUA

Estelí

Jinotega

Chinadega   Matagalpa

León

Managua   Masaya

Granada

Rivas   Lake
                   Nicaragua

Caribbean
Sea

Pacific Ocean

COSTA RICA

PANAMA

Introduction

A revolution is unfolding in Nicaragua. Led by the fighters of the Sandinista National Liberation Front (FSLN), the workers and peasants of that country carried out a victorious insurrection against the brutal and corrupt U.S.-installed Somoza dictatorship and took into their own hands the power to shape their destiny. The July 19, 1979, downfall of the dictatorship marked the beginning of a new stage in the history of Nicaragua, one that has seen big changes and that holds the promise of even bigger changes in the future.

From the start, the U.S. government resisted these changes. As it became apparent that even increased military aid could not save the personal dictatorship of Anastasio Somoza, Washington maneuvered to find a solution that would leave intact Somoza's military force, the hated National Guard. When that failed, first Carter and then Reagan used promises of aid and later military threats and paramilitary attacks in an effort to slow down and overturn Nicaragua's revolution.

The U.S. has stationed warships off Nicaragua's coast. It plans to construct new military airfields in neighboring Honduras. In violation of U.S. laws, it has given the green light to military training of remnants of Somoza's National Guard and other counterrevolutionaries at private camps in Florida and California. And the CIA has trained, armed, and supplied several thousand Somozaist counterrevolutionaries and mercenaries stationed along Nicaragua's border in Honduras. In early 1982, it was reported that the National Security Council had budgeted at least $19 million to promote destabilizing and covert actions — including terrorist attacks — against the Nicaraguan people and government.

Washington's propaganda campaign against the Nicaraguan revolution charges that the revolution is undemocratic, that it has meant economic disaster for Nicaragua, that the Nicaraguans seek to export their revolution by force, and that the leaders of the revolution — the cadres of the FSLN — are simply agents of Cuba, and that their revolution was "made in Havana." As the speeches in this collection show, these are outright lies.

While the example of revolutionary Cuba is a tremendous inspiration to struggling people around the world, the insurrection that triumphed in July 1979, and the revolutionary changes that have occurred since, came out of the decades-long struggle of the Nicaraguan people to free themselves from foreign domination and to determine their own destiny. Nicaraguans have a proud tradition of resisting attempts to make Nicaragua the United States backyard.

For Central Americans, the Monroe Doctrine and its subsequent refinements meant not freedom from foreign intervention, but exactly the opposite. As the speeches collected here explain, the U.S. rulers maintained order and stability in their Central American neocolonies through repeated landings of the Marines.

In this century, the Nicaraguan most closely associated with the struggle against U.S. domination was Gen. Augusto César Sandino. In 1927 he organized an army of workers and peasants to drive out the U.S. Marines, who had again occupied Nicaragua in 1926. Sandino's Army for the Defense of National Sovereignty fought them for seven years and won tremendous popular support. When the Marines were finally withdrawn in 1933, they left behind them as a replacement force the infamous National Guard headed by Anastasio Somoza García. This military force was to be the guarantor of stability for the U.S. in Nicaragua. One of its first acts, on February 21, 1934, was to murder Sandino, who had agreed to a cease-fire after the withdrawal of the Marines. From that time on, the National Guard, headed by a succession of Somozas, became notorious the world over for its brutality and corruption.

Using this power, the Somozas built themselves a fortune estimated, in 1979, at $400-500 million. They controlled the only two meatpacking plants with export licenses, half the sugar mills, two-thirds of the commercial fishing, 40 percent of rice production, and the largest milk-processing plant. They dominated cement manufacture, owned the national steamship and airline companies, a newspaper, two TV stations, and a radio station.

They did all of this with Washington's blessing. As President Franklin D. Roosevelt once said, "Somoza may be a son of a bitch, but he's our son of a bitch." Nicaragua was repeatedly used by U.S. imperialism as a base for intervention throughout the area. CIA invasions both of Guatemala in 1954 and of Cuba in 1961 were based there.

The great wealth of the Somozas was amassed at the cost of great suffering for the Nicaraguan people. Under Somoza half the population was illiterate. Infant mortality was so high that in poor neighborhoods one-third of all children died before age one. Life expectancy was only fifty years.

Eighty percent of the population of Managua, the capital, lacked running water and only one house in ten had a decent roof. Half the sick received no medical care at all.

Inequitable distribution of the land meant that many went hungry. Half of all the farmland was owned by less than 2 percent of the landowners, while the poorest 50 percent of the farmers held less than 4 percent of the land. For these farmers, the average annual income in 1972 was only $35.

These terrible conditions led to widespread opposition to the dictatorship and a continual struggle against the regime and its North American backers.

Out of this tradition of struggle, the FSLN was born. Carlos Fonseca Amador, Tomás Borge, and Silvio Mayorga, veterans of the student struggle of the 1950s, joined with others including a veteran of Sandino's army, Colonel Santos López, in July 1961, taking their inspiration both from Sandino's struggle and from the successful Cuban revolution of 1959.

The struggle the FSLN began then, with a guerilla front along the northern border, was to last until the insurrection. It took many different forms. The Sandinistas worked clandestinely and, when possible, legally; they worked in the mountains and in the cities; in the villages and in the factories. Many were arrested, tortured, and killed. But they persevered. They won the respect, confidence, and loyalty of almost the entire population, so that when the insurrection finally triumphed they could truly be described as the legitimate representatives of the Nicaraguan people.

Immediately after the overthrow of Somoza, the FSLN began to implement its program for Nicaragua's reconstruction, and this won them even broader support from the workers and peasants. For the first time, a government responsive to the needs of the oppressed was in power.

The revolutionary government launched a literacy campaign to teach the people how to read and write. It confiscated the property of Somoza and his closest collaborators, bringing about 25 percent of the cultivable land under government control. It nationalized the banks and sought to use their resources to rebuild the devastation caused by Somoza's National Guard. It encouraged workers to form unions and enforced workers' rights, such as the eight-hour day, paid vacations, and social security protection. It helped organize workers in many plants into production committees and took additional steps to increase workers' participation in planning production and managing factories. It intervened through nationalizations against capitalists who sought to undermine the revolution by decapitalizing their enterprises or otherwise restricting production.

All these actions have earned the FSLN and Nicaragua's revolutionary government increased prestige and authority in Nicaragua and around the world. These actions have also earned the Nicaraguans the enmity of the United States government.

Washington's interests are irreconcilably opposed to those of the workers and peasants of Nicaragua. It has an enormous political and economic stake in maintaining the low wages, substandard living conditions, and brutal dictatorships that are imposed on the working people of Central America. And it fears that the Nicaraguan revolution will set a powerful example for the oppressed and exploited everywhere.

*   *   *

The speeches, documents, and interviews collected here are by five central leaders of the FSLN. Carlos Fonseca Amador, one of the founders of the FSLN, was its central leader until he was murdered by the Somoza dictatorship in 1976. Tomás Borge, Daniel Ortega, Humberto Ortega, and Jaime Wheelock are all members of the FSLN's National Directorate and play major roles in the Government of National Reconstruction. Together their writings and speeches give a picture of how the Nicaraguan revolution developed and where it is headed. In this collection the leaders of the FSLN speak for themselves, and that is the best answer to the slanders and lies circulated by Washington.

We can learn a great deal from the Nicaraguan workers and peasants and their leaders. At the very time that workers in the U.S. are being thrown out of their jobs, social services are being slashed, and new restrictions are being imposed on our democratic rights, our brothers and sisters in Nicaragua are taking gigantic steps forward.

One clear example is in education. While the Democrats' and Republicans' cuts in aid for schooling are increasingly making education the province of the wealthy, the Nicaraguans have enrolled one-third of their population — almost 900,000 — in some kind of formal study. Similarly, while hospitals and clinics are being closed in major U.S. cities, the Nicaraguans are busy building new medical care facilities throughout the country and have increased their expenditures for health care six times. Outlays for all social services in Nicaragua doubled from 1978 to 1981. While the U.S. rulers carry out bipartisan policies that foster unemployment and plant shutdowns, the FSLN and the Government of National Reconstruction are putting Nicaragua back to work.

These enormous differences result from the fact that the workers and peasants of Nicaragua now have a government that represents and fights for *their* interests, not those of a ruling rich. The example they are providing for workers in North America and around the world of the kinds of immediate social gains that are possible when political power is in the hands of working people is what Washington really fears.

The advances of the Nicaraguan workers and peasants deserve not only our maximum efforts to stop intervention by the U.S. and its allies against the revolution, but also our careful study so that we can learn from their experiences.

Bruce Marcus
April 1982

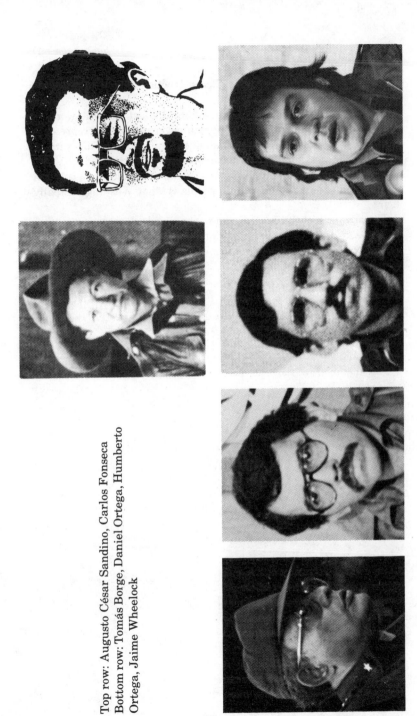

Top row: Augusto César Sandino, Carlos Fonseca
Bottom row: Tomás Borge, Daniel Ortega, Humberto
Ortega, Jaime Wheelock

The Historic Program of the FSLN

*This document was first presented to the Nicaraguan people in 1969.
It was reprinted by the FSLN Department of Propaganda and Political
Education in June 1981. This translation from that edition is by Will
Reissner.*

The Sandinista National Liberation Front (FSLN) arose out of the
Nicaraguan people's need to have a "vanguard organization" capable
of taking political power through direct struggle against its enemies
and establishing a social system that wipes out the exploitation and
poverty that our people have been subjected to in past history.

The FSLN is a politico-military organization, whose strategic objective is to take political power by destroying the military and bureaucratic apparatus of the dictatorship and to establish a revolutionary
government based on the worker-peasant alliance and the conver-
gence of all the patriotic anti-imperialist and anti-oligarchic forces in
the country.

The people of Nicaragua suffer under subjugation to a reactionary
and fascist clique imposed by Yankee imperialism in 1932, the year
Anastasio Somoza García was named commander in chief of the so-
called National Guard (GN).

The Somozaist clique has reduced Nicaragua to the status of a neocolony exploited by the Yankee monopolies and the country's oligarchic groups.

The present regime is politically unpopular and juridically illegal.
The recognition and aid it gets from the North Americans is irrefut-
able proof of foreign interference in the affairs of Nicaragua.

The FSLN has seriously and with great responsibility analyzed the
national reality and has resolved to confront the dictatorship with
arms in hand. We have concluded that the triumph of the Sandinista
people's revolution and the overthrow of the regime that is an enemy
of the people will take place through the development of a hard-fought
and prolonged people's war.

Whatever maneuvers and resources Yankee imperialism deploys,
the Somozaist dictatorship is condemned to total failure in the face of

the rapid advance and development of the people's forces, headed by the Sandinista National Liberation Front.

Given this historic conjuncture the FSLN has worked out this political program with an eye to strengthening and developing our organization, inspiring and stimulating the people of Nicaragua to march forward with the resolve to fight until the dictatorship is overthrown and to resist the intervention of Yankee imperialism, in order to forge a free, prosperous, and revolutionary homeland.

I. A revolutionary government

The Sandinista people's revolution will establish a revolutionary government that will eliminate the reactionary structure that arose from rigged elections and military coups, and the people's power will create a Nicaragua that is free of exploitation, oppression, backwardness; a free, progressive, and independent country.

The revolutionary government will apply the following measures of a political character:

A. It will endow revolutionary power with a structure that allows the full participation of the entire people, on the national level as well as the local level (departmental, municipal, neighborhood).

B. It will guarantee that all citizens can fully exercise all individual freedoms and it will respect human rights.

C. It will guarantee the free exchange of ideas, which above all leads to vigorously broadening the people's rights and national rights.

D. It will guarantee freedom for the worker-union movement to organize in the city and countryside; and freedom to organize peasant, youth, student, women's, cultural, sporting, and similar groups.

E. It will guarantee the right of emigrant and exiled Nicaraguans to return to their native soil.

F. It will guarantee the right to asylum for citizens of other countries who are persecuted for participation in the revolutionary struggle.

G. It will severely punish the gangsters who are guilty of persecuting, informing on, abusing, torturing, or murdering revolutionaries and the people.

H. Those individuals who occupy high political posts as a result of rigged elections and military coups will be stripped of their political rights.

The revolutionary government will apply the following measures of an economic character:

A. It will expropriate the landed estates, factories, companies, buildings, means of transportation, and other wealth usurped by the Somoza family and accumulated through the misappropriation and plunder of the nation's wealth.

B. It will expropriate the landed estates, factories, companies, means of transportation, and other wealth usurped by the politicians and military officers, and all other accomplices, who have taken advantage of the present regime's administrative corruption.

C. It will nationalize the wealth of all the foreign companies that exploit the mineral, forest, maritime, and other kinds of resources.

D. It will establish workers' control over the administrative management of the factories and other wealth that are expropriated and nationalized.

E. It will centralize the mass transit service.

F. It will nationalize the banking system, which will be placed at the exclusive service of the country's economic development.

G. It will establish an independent currency.

H. It will refuse to honor the loans imposed on the country by the Yankee monopolies or those of any other power.

I. It will establish commercial relations with all countries, whatever their system, to benefit the country's economic development.

J. It will establish a suitable taxation policy, which will be applied with strict justice.

K. It will prohibit usury. This prohibition will apply to Nicaraguan nationals as well as foreigners.

L. It will protect the small and medium-size owners (producers, merchants) while restricting the excesses that lead to the exploitation of the workers.

M. It will establish state control over foreign trade, with an eye to diversifying it and making it independent.

N. It will rigorously restrict the importation of luxury items.

O. It will plan the national economy, putting an end to the anarchy characteristic of the capitalist system of production. An important part of this planning will focus on the industrialization and electrification of the country.

II. The agrarian revolution

The Sandinista people's revolution will work out an agrarian policy that achieves an authentic agrarian reform; a reform that will, in the immediate term, carry out massive distribution of the land, eliminating the land grabs by the large landlords in favor of the workers (small producers) who labor on the land.

A. It will expropriate and eliminate the capitalist and feudal estates.

B. It will turn over the land to the peasants, free of charge, in accordance with the principle that the land should belong to those who work it.

C. It will carry out a development plan for livestock raising aimed at diversifying and increasing the productivity of that sector.

D. It will guarantee the peasants the following rights:
1. Timely and adequate agricultural credit.
2. Marketability (a guaranteed market for their production).
3. Technical assistance.

E. It will protect the patriotic landowners who collaborate with the guerrilla struggle, by paying them for their landholdings that exceed the limit established by the revolutionary government.

F. It will stimulate and encourage the peasants to organize themselves in cooperatives, so they can take their destiny into their own hands and directly participate in the development of the country.

G. It will abolish the debts the peasantry incurred to the landlord and any type of usurer.

H. It will eliminate the forced idleness that exists for most of the year in the countryside, and it will be attentive to creating sources of jobs for the peasant population.

III. Revolution in culture and education

The Sandinista people's revolution will establish the bases for the development of the national culture, the people's education, and university reform.

A. It will push forward a massive campaign to immediately wipe out "illiteracy."

B. It will develop the national culture and will root out the neocolonial penetration in our culture.

C. It will rescue the progressive intellectuals, and their works that have arisen throughout our history, from the neglect in which they have been maintained by the anti-people's regimes.

D. It will give attention to the development and progress of education at the various levels (primary, intermediate, technical, university, etc.), and education will be free at all levels and obligatory at some.

E. It will grant scholarships at various levels of education to students who have limited economic resources. The scholarships will include housing, food, clothing, books, and transportation.

F. It will train more and better teachers who have the scientific knowledge that the present era requires, to satisfy the needs of our entire student population.

G. It will nationalize the centers of private education that have been immorally turned into industries by merchants who hypocritically invoke religious principles.

H. It will adapt the teaching programs to the needs of the country; it will apply teaching methods to the scientific and research needs of the country.

I. It will carry out a university reform that will include, among other things, the following measures:

1. It will rescue the university from the domination of the exploiting classes, so it can serve the real creators and shapers of our culture: the people. University instruction must be oriented around man, around the people. The university must stop being a breeding ground for bureaucratic egotists.

2. Eliminate the discrimination in access to university classes suffered by youth from the working class and peasantry.

3. Increase the state budget for the university so there are the economic resources to solve the various problems confronting it.

4. Majority student representation on the boards of the faculties, keeping in mind that the student body is the main segment of the university population.

5. Eliminate the neocolonial penetration of the university, especially the penetration by the North American monopolies through the charity donations of the pseudophilanthropic foundations.

6. Promotion of free, experimental, scientific investigation that must contribute to dealing with national and universal questions.

7. Strengthen the unity of the students, faculty, and investigators with the whole people, by perpetuating the selfless example of the students and intellectuals who have offered their lives for the sake of the patriotic ideal.

IV. Labor legislation and social security

The Sandinista people's revolution will eliminate the injustices of the living and working conditions suffered by the working class under the brutal exploitation, and will institute labor legislation and social assistance.

A. It will enact a labor code that will regulate, among other things, the following rights:

1. It will adopt the principle that "those who don't work don't eat," of course making exceptions for those who are unable to partici-

pate in the process of production due to age (children, old people), medical condition, or other reasons beyond their control.

2. Strict enforcement of the eight-hour work day.

3. The income of the workers (wages and other benefits) must be sufficient to satisfy their daily needs.

4. Respect for the dignity of the worker, prohibiting and punishing unjust treatment of workers in the course of their labor.

5. Abolition of unjustified firings.

6. Obligation to pay wages in the period required by law.

7. Right of all workers to periodic vacations.

B. It will eliminate the scourge of unemployment.

C. It will extend the scope of the social security system to all the workers and public employees in the country. The scope will include coverage for illness, physical incapacity, and retirement.

D. It will provide free medical assistance to the entire population. It will set up clinics and hospitals throughout the national territiory.

E. It will undertake massive campaigns to eradicate endemic illnesses and prevent epidemics.

F. It will carry out urban reform, which will provide each family with adequate shelter. It will put an end to profiteering speculation in urban land (subdivisions, urban construction, rental housing) that exploits the need that working families in the cities have for an adequate roof over their heads in order to live.

G. It will initiate and expand the construction of adequate housing for the peasant population.

H. It will reduce the charges for water, light, sewers, urban beautification; it will apply programs to extend all these services to the entire urban and rural population.

I. It will encourage participation in sports of all types and categories.

J. It will eliminate the humiliation of begging by putting the abovementioned measures into practice.

V. Administrative honesty

The Sandinista people's revolution will root out administrative governmental corruption, and will establish strict administrative honesty.

A. It will abolish the criminal vice industry (prostitution, gambling, drug use, etc.) which the privileged sector of the National Guard and the foreign parasites exploit.

B. It will establish strict control over the collection of taxes to prevent government functionaries from profiting, putting an end to the normal practice of the present regime's official agencies.

C. It will end the arbitrary actions of the members of the GN, who plunder the population through the subterfuge of local taxes.

D. It will put an end to the situation wherein military commanders appropriate the budget that is supposed to go to take care of common prisoners, and it will establish centers designed to rehabilitate these wrongdoers.

E. It will abolish the smuggling that is practiced on a large scale by the gang of politicians, officers, and foreigners who are the regime's accomplices.

F. It will severely punish persons who engage in crimes against administrative honesty (embezzlement, smuggling, trafficking in vices, etc.), using greatest severity when it involves elements active in the revolutionary movement.

VI. Reincorporation of the Atlantic Coast

The Sandinista people's revolution will put into practice a special plan for the Atlantic Coast, which has been abandoned to total neglect, in order to incorporate this area into the nation's life.

A. It will end the unjust exploitation the Atlantic Coast has suffered throughout history by the foreign monopolies, especially Yankee imperialism.

B. It will prepare suitable lands in the zone for the development of agriculture and ranching.

C. It will establish conditions that encourage the development of the fishing and forest industries.

D. It will encourage the flourishing of this region's local cultural values, which flow from the specific aspects of its historic tradition.

E. It will wipe out the odious discrimination to which the indigenous Miskitos, Sumos, Zambos, and Blacks of this region are subjected.

VII. Emancipation of women

The Sandinista people's revolution will abolish the odious discrimination that women have been subjected to compared to men; it will establish economic, political, and cultural equality between woman and man.

A. It will pay special attention to the mother and child.

B. It will eliminate prostitution and other social vices, through which the dignity of women will be raised.

C. It will put an end to the system of servitude that women suffer, which is reflected in the tragedy of the abandoned working mother.

D. It will establish for children born out of wedlock the right to equal protection by the revolutionary institutions.

E. It will establish daycare centers for the care and attention of the children of working women.

F. It will establish a two-month maternity leave before and after birth for women who work.

G. It will raise women's political, cultural, and vocational levels through their participation in the revolutionary process.

VIII. Respect for religious beliefs

The Sandinista people's revolution will guarantee the population of believers the freedom to profess any religion.

A. It will respect the right of citizens to profess and practice any religious belief.

B. It will support the work of priests and other religious figures who defend the working people.

IX. Independent foreign policy

The Sandinista people's revolution will eliminate the foreign policy of submission to Yankee imperialism, and will establish a patriotic foreign policy of absolute national independence and one that is for authentic universal peace.

A. It will put an end to the Yankee interference in the internal problems of Nicaragua and will practice a policy of mutual respect with other countries and fraternal collaboration between peoples.

B. It will expel the Yankee military mission, the so-called Peace Corps (spies in the guise of technicians), and military and similar political elements who constitute a barefaced intervention in the country.

C. It will accept economic and technical aid from any country, but always and only when this does not involve political compromises.

D. Together with other peoples of the world it will promote a campaign in favor of authentic universal peace.

E. It will abrogate all treaties, signed with any foreign power, that damage national sovereignty.

X. Central American people's unity

The Sandinista people's revolution is for the true union of the Central American peoples in a single country.

A. It will support authentic unity with the fraternal peoples of Central America. This unity will lead the way to coordinating the efforts to achieve national liberation and establish a new system without imperialist domination or national betrayal.

B. It will eliminate the so-called integration, whose aim is to increase Central America's submission to the North American monopolies and the local reactionary forces.

XI. Solidarity among peoples

The Sandinista people's revolution will put an end to the use of the national territory as a base for Yankee aggression against other fraternal peoples and will put into practice militant solidarity with fraternal peoples fighting for their liberation.

A. It will actively support the struggle of the peoples of Asia, Africa, and Latin America against the new and old colonialism and against the common enemy: Yankee imperialism.

B. It will support the struggle of the Black people and all the people of the United States for an authentic democracy and equal rights.

C. It will support the struggle of all peoples against the establishment of Yankee military bases in foreign countries.

XII. People's patriotic army

The Sandinista people's revolution will abolish the armed force called the National Guard, which is an enemy of the people, and will create a patriotic, revolutionary, and people's army.

A. It will abolish the National Guard, a force that is an enemy of the people, created by the North American occupation forces in 1927 to pursue, torture, and murder the Sandinista patriots.

B. In the new people's army, professional soldiers who are members of the old army will be able to play a role providing they have observed the following conduct:

1. They have supported the guerrilla struggle.

2. They have not participated in murder, plunder, torture, and persecution of the people and the revolutionary activists.

3. They have rebelled against the despotic and dynastic regime of the Somozas.

C. It will strengthen the new people's army, raising its fighting ability and its tactical and technical level.

D. It will inculcate in the consciousness of the members of the people's army the principle of basing themselves on their own forces in the fulfillment of their duties and the development of all their creative activity.

E. It will deepen the revolutionary ideals of the members of the people's army with an eye toward strengthening their patriotic spirit and their firm conviction to fight until victory is achieved, overcoming obstacles and correcting errors.

F. It will forge a conscious discipline in the ranks of the people's army and will encourage the close ties that must exist between the combatants and the people.

G. It will establish obligatory military service and will arm the students, workers, and farmers, who — organized in people's militias — will defend the rights won against the inevitable attack by the reactionary forces of the country and Yankee imperialism.

XIII. Veneration of our martyrs

The Sandinista people's revolution will maintain eternal gratitude to and veneration of our homeland's martyrs and will continue the shining example of heroism and selflessness they have bequeathed to us.

A. It will educate the new generations in eternal gratitude and veneration toward those who have fallen in the struggle to make Nicaragua a free homeland.

B. It will establish a secondary school to educate the children of our people's martrys.

C. It will inculcate in the entire people the imperishable example of our marytrs, defending the revolutionary ideal: Ever onward to victory!!!

Nicaragua: Zero Hour

by Carlos Fonseca Amador

*Carlos Fonseca Amador was the central leader of the FSLN from the
time he helped found it in July 1961 until his murder by the Somoza
dictatorship on November 8, 1976. As a student, Fonseca had joined the
pro-Moscow Nicaraguan Socialist Party, with which he later came into
political conflict. First arrested for his revolutionary activities in 1954,
Fonseca was repeatedly detained. In 1969, after an escape from a Costa
Rican jail, he went to Cuba, where he published this article he had written earlier in the year. It first appeared in the Spanish-language edition
of* Tricontinental, *no. 14, 1969. This translation, by Michael Taber
and Will Reissner, is based on a 1979 reprinting of the article by the
National Secretariat of Propaganda and Political Education of the
FSLN.*

The economic situation

The people of Nicaragua have been suffering under the yoke of a
reactionary clique imposed by Yankee imperialism virtually since
1932, the year in which Anastasio Somoza G. was named commander
in chief of the so-called National Guard (GN), a post that had previously been filled by Yankee officials. This clique has reduced Nicaragua
to the status of a neocolony — exploited by the Yankee monopolies and
the local capitalist class.

At the present time, the economic crisis that the country has been
suffering has gotten worse. In the years immediately preceding 1966,
the national economy grew at an annual rate of 8 percent. By contrast,
in the years 1966 and 1967 the growth rate declined to 3.1 and 4.6 percent respectively.

The production of cotton, which has been increasing since 1950, will
increase only slightly in the future. This is due, on the one hand, to a
saturation of the foreign capitalist market supplied by national production. And in addition, it is due to the growing competition from
synthetic fibers. There has, in fact, been a major drop in the prices of-

fered by the foreign capitalist market for the harvest from the 1968 planting. This last fact has persuaded the country's government to establish commercial relations with some socialist countries, which will take part of the cotton harvest. This crop amounts to 26 percent of the cultivated land in Nicaragua.

Regarding coffee, which is the second largest export product, there is already overproduction, which cannot be sold on the capitalist market. Regarding sugar production, official sources state that it is unlikely that the pace of growth can be maintained in the immediate future.

The exploitation of minerals such as gold and copper, which is directly in the hands of foreign investors, pays ridiculously small sums to the national treasury through taxes. Parallel with this, the handing over of the national riches to the Yankee monopolies has continued to increase. In 1967, for example, a law went into effect that gave Magnavox, a company specializing in the exploitation of forests, absolute ownership of a million hectares of national territory.*

At the same time, the ruling clique handles the funds of the state banks as if they were personal funds, while fraud and smuggling reach staggering dimensions. The Somoza family, which had very limited economic resources when it took power, has obtained a vast fiefdom, whose domains go beyond Nicaragua's borders and extend into the other countries of Central America.

In Nicaragua, moreover, there is an unjust distribution of land. Statistical reports for the year 1952 show that a few proprietors control 55 percent of the total area of privately owned farms.

Nicaragua offers exceptional conditions for the development of cattle raising. Nevertheless, the consumption of products derived from cattle has declined and the increase in exports has largely been due to foreign sales of cows that would have contributed to an increase in the quantity of animals.

The advantages provided to producers of products for foreign markets — in this case for growing cotton — has led to a situation where food products are grown on the worst lands, which also means that imports are needed to satisfy this important sector.

Nicaragua is among the countries that have been hurt most by the so-called Central American economic integration. It is well-known that this integration has been simply a plan to increase the economic hold of the Yankee monopolies over Central America. This scandalous fact has reached such a magnitude that even spokesmen of the Nicaraguan regime itself have been put in the situation of publicly stating

*1 hectare = 2.47 acres

that the industries established as a result of this integration do not enhance national economic development.

As with the other countries of Central America, there is no oil production in Nicaragua. It has been stated, however, that if there were possibilities for oil exploitation in Central America, the Yankee monopolies would have an interest in hiding it, in order to maintain it as a reserve in case revolutionary governments were established in the countries that currently produce oil.

Although the governmental capitalist sector represents the dominant segment of the country's capitalist class, it must be pointed out that the sector of capitalists who call themselves "oppositionists" are also involved in exploiting the Nicaraguan people. Many times, the governing and "opposition" groups jointly exploit important sectors of the national economy, as is the case regarding sugar, milk, the press, banking, liquor distilleries, etc.

The economic system described above turns the other classes making up Nicaragua's population into victims of exploitation and oppression. The poor diet of the working classes has caused numerous deaths through hunger. It's known that in 1964 hundreds of peasants died of hunger in the Tempisque area, in the department of Matagalpa. In various regions in the north, the incidence of goiters is very high. In the Malacaguas area, there have been cases of collective dementia provoked by poor diet; night blindness resulting from Vitamin A and protein deficiencies has occurred in areas around the town of Darío.

A few years ago, some tests carried out in a school in Jinotepes, a region located near the country's capital, indicated that every one of the 200 students suffered tuberculosis.

Only 1.1 percent of the Nicaraguan population has completed primary school. Fifty percent of the population has had no schooling whatever. The proportion of students that leave school in the first grade or repeat grades is extremely high (73 percent). Only 21 percent of the student population comes from the sector of society with income levels at or below the country's average. Out of 200,000 young people from fourteen to nineteen years of age, barely 20,000 are enrolled in high school or commercial, vocational, or agricultural education.

Infant mortality reaches dreadful levels in Nicaragua. More than 50 percent of the deaths in the country occur among persons under fourteen years of age. Out of every thousand children born, 102 die. Six out of every ten deaths are caused by infectious — meaning curable — diseases. In recent investigations 9.28 percent of the population had a positive reaction in tests for malaria, while in Costa Rica it is 0.96 percent, and in Panama, 4.98 percent.

Nicaragua: A victim of Yankee aggression
for more than a century

To understand Nicaragua's current political situation it's necessary to keep in mind certain characteristics that have been seen throughout its national history. Nicaragua is a country that has suffered foreign aggression and oppression for more than four centuries. Together with the other countries of Latin America, Nicaragua faced rule by the Iberian peninsula. In a region of its territory located on the Atlantic Coast, it also suffered British domination, which lasted for 150 years until 1893. At the same time, Nicaragua was among the first victims of the aggressive policy of the United States.

Shortly after the so-called Monroe Doctrine was proclaimed by the U.S. government in 1823, Nicaragua was chosen as the target of Yankee rapacity.

In the decade of the 1830s, representatives of the Washington government traveled through Nicaragua in order to obtain information to prepare for intervention in the country.

Below is a list of some of the Yankee acts of aggression that Nicaragua has suffered:

1850. The governments of England and the United States sign the so-called Clayton-Bulwer treaty, by which these powers, without taking the Nicaraguan government into account, arbitrarily decide to divide among themselves the right to build an interocean route through Nicaragua.

1854. In June of that year, a U.S. warship commanded by a seaman named Hollins, bombards the Nicaraguan port of San Juan del Norte and reduces it to ashes.

1855. Several thousand North American filibusters, headed by William Walker, intervene in Nicaragua. Walker proclaims himself president of Nicaragua and is recognized as such by the Yankee government of Franklin Pierce. Among other savage measures, he decrees slavery. The Nicaraguan people, with the backing of the other peoples of Central America, take up arms and succeed in throwing out the interventionists.

1870. The Nicaraguan government's head of foreign relations, Dr. Tomás Ayón, sends patriotic notes to the U.S. government representative, in which he protests that government's interference in the internal affairs of Nicaragua and demands reparation for the material damages caused by the bombardment of 1854 and fulfillment of financal commitments made by the millionaire investor Cornelius Vanderbilt.

1893. Lewis Hanke, representative of the U.S. government, is unsuccessful in his attempt to intervene on behalf of a reactionary group, against whom a resolute, popular rebellion occurs.

1907. U.S. government warships occupy the waters of the Gulf of Fonseca.

1909. The nationalist Nicaraguan government shoots two North Americans named Cannon and Groce, who were guilty of participating in armed actions against the Nicaraguan government. The U.S. government, through the U.S. secretary of state, sends a note to the Nicaraguan government, known as the "Knox note," in which it openly states that it has the right to intervene in Nicaragua's internal affairs.

1910. U.S. warships intervene on the side of the Conservatives who are in revolt against the Nicaraguan government. In this way, the U.S. imposes a sell-out government on Nicaragua.

1912. The country is occupied by thousands of U.S. Marines. Armed resistance to the occupation lasts for several months, at the end of which the patriotic leader Benjamín Zaledón dies with arms in hand.

1914. Emiliano Chamorro, the Conservative government's ambassador to the United States, and U.S. Secretary of State Bryan sign the disgraceful canal treaty known as the Chamorro-Bryan pact.

1927. José María Moncada, a representative of the Liberal bourgeoisie and military head of the people's army that has been fighting the government imposed by the North American intervention, commits a betrayal and enters into agreement with the representative of the State Department, Henry L. Stimson, who years later would become secretary of war in the Truman government. While Stimson occupied this post, the barbaric atomic bombing of Hiroshima and Nagasaki took place.

Augusto César Sandino, head of a column of the people's army, refuses to accept the Moncada agreement and rises up in arms against the North American occupation and the traitors who support it. The Army for the Defense of National Sovereignty, headed by Sandino, carries out more than 500 clashes with the occupation forces. This makes it impossible for the Yankee occupiers to defeat the Nicaraguan patriots militarily, but before leaving the country at the beginning of 1933, they leave behind them a reactionary force called the National Guard.

1934. On February 21 of that year, Augusto César Sandino is murdered. Anastasio Somoza G., commander in chief of the National Guard orders this crime carried out after receiving instructions from the Yankee Ambassador Arthur Bliss Lane. The murder is carried out during the days when Augusto César Sandino and his comrades were preparing to fight against the antipopular direction in which the country was being led. Having received guarantees that his life would be respected, Sandino decided to take part in talks in order to dispel the slanderous charge that he was not interested in peace.

1936. Somoza ousts the constitutional president of the country, with the approval of the U.S. government.

1947. Somoza ousts the constitutional president of the country, again with the approval of the U.S. government.

1960. The U.S. fleet in the Caribbean Sea is mobilized to protect the governments of Guatemala and Nicaragua, which are facing growing popular discontent.

Nicaragua: A base for Yankee aggression

Together with plundering its national riches, U.S. imperialism has been using Nicaragua's geographic position to make it a base for aggression against other Latin American peoples.

The Chamorro-Bryan canal treaty is still in force, which practically makes the U.S. Nicaragua's master. This treaty authorizes the Washington government to build military bases in Nicaragua, and also grants it the right to build an interocean canal through the country.

Below is a list of various events showing how Nicaragua serves as a base for imperialist aggression against other Latin American peoples, and especially against the countries around the Caribbean Sea:

1948. With its armed forces the Somoza government intervenes in Costa Rican territory, where an armed conflict is developing that culminates in the persecution of that country's workers' movement.

1954. The Somoza government supports the Guatemalan mercenaries that launch an attack against the democratic government of Jacobo Arbenz.

1955. The Somoza government intervenes militarily in Costa Rica.

1961. The mercenary invasion that is defeated by revolutionary Cuba at the Bay of Pigs leaves from Puerto Cabezas in Nicaragua.

1965. National Guard troops form part of the foreign forces that, led by U.S. Marines, occupy the territory of the Dominican Republic. In the same year, 1965, counterrevolutionary mercenaries captured in Cuba state that they left from training camps in Nicaraguan territory.

1966. René Schick, nominal president of Nicaragua, states while traveling in the United States that Nicaraguan territory can be used as a base for forces aimed against Cuba.

1967. Anastasio Somoza Debayle makes known his decision to send members of the National Guard to take part in the aggression in Vietnam.

1968. It has been asserted that Somoza's agents took part in the overthrow of the government of Arnulfo Arias,* who despite his submissiveness, apparently didn't fully satisfy all the demands of the U.S. government.

A tradition of rebellion

A notable feature of Nicaraguan history, particularly during the stage that began with independence from Spanish rule in 1821, is the use of violence by different political forces within the exploiting classes, fighting over control of the government. Peaceful changes between different factions of the ruling classes, which have been rather frequent in other Latin American countries, have not taken place in Nicaragua. This traditional experience predisposed the Nicaraguan people against electoral farces and in favor of armed struggle. There is no doubt, then, that the Nicaraguan people have a rich tradition of rebellion.

It is a fact that the Nicaraguan people have taken up arms to fight specific forms of oppression many times through movements headed by individuals, movements that in no sense could lead to progressive revolutionary change. This represents another characteristic of the Nicaraguan people throughout their history. This characteristic relates to the lack of a deepgoing revolutionary consciousness.

The ideological obscurantism inherited from the colonial epoch has continued to weigh heavily in preventing the people from marching with full consciousness toward struggle for social change. It is indisputable that throughout their history the Nicaraguan people have endured numerous battles in which they have demonstrated their courage. But they have marched to these struggles more by instinct than through consciousness. Perhaps it is useful to repeat in the case of Nicaragua the words that Marx wrote in relation to Spain. Marx pointed out that the Spanish people had traditionally been a rebel people, but not a revolutionary people.

The national and international conditions that currently prevail make it possible for at least a sector of the Nicaraguan people to initiate armed struggle, conscious that they are trying not simply to achieve a change of men in power, but a change of the system — the overthrow of the exploiting classes and the victory of the exploited classes.

*Arnulfo Arias, president of Panama, was deposed by a military coup eleven days after his election in October 1968.

Origin and prolongation of the present regime

It is not possible to analyze the conditions that have permitted the ruling clique to remain in power for more than three decades without stopping to study the country's situation at the time this regime was installed, as well as the situation that has been developing for more than thirty years.

From 1926 to 1936 the Nicaraguan people went through one of the most intense periods in their history. The armed struggle, through which the people sought change, produced more than 20,000 deaths. The struggle began as a fight against a Conservative government imposed by the North Americans, went through the Sandinista resistance, and concluded with Anastasio Somoza's military coup against Juan B. Sacasa.

The struggle was carried out without an industrial proletariat existing. The incipient bourgeoisie betrayed the Nicaraguan people and sold out to the Yankee intervention. The bourgeoisie could not be immediately replaced as the vanguard of the people's struggle by a revolutionary proletariat. The Sandinista resistance, which became the heroic vanguard of the people, had an almost totally peasant composition, and therein lies the glory and the tragedy of that revolutionary movement.

It was a glory for the Nicaraguan people that the most humble class responded to the stains against the honor of the homeland, and at the same time a tragedy because it involved a peasantry lacking any political level whatsoever. Moreover, there were leaders of important guerrilla columns who were totally illiterate. As a result, once Sandino was assassinated his movement could not maintain its continuity.

The prolonged armed struggle, which ended in betrayal and frustration, exhausted the people's strength. The sector headed by Anastasio Somoza won hegemony over the traditional Liberal Party, while the opposition to Somoza's government came to be dominated by the traditional Conservative Party, a reactionary political force profoundly weakened because in the 1930s this party's sell-out to the Yankee interventionists was fresh in the people's memory.

An important factor that also seriously contributed to the interruption of the anti-imperialist struggle was the situation arising from the outbreak of the Second World War, which concentrated the focus of the world's reactionaries on Europe and Asia. Yankee imperialism, the traditional enemy of the Nicaraguan people, became an ally of the world antifascist front. The lack of a revolutionary leadership in Nicaragua prevented this reality from being interpreted correctly, and

Somoza took advantage of the situation to consolidate the rule of his clique.

The rise of the old Marxist sector

For many years, the influence of the Marxist sector in the opposition was almost completely under the control of the Conservative sector, the political force representing the interests of one sector of the capitalist class. One of the factors that contributed to the weakness of the Marxist sector originated in the conditions in which the Nicaraguan Socialist Party (the traditional Communist organization in Nicaragua) was formed. That organization was formed in June 1944, when the Second World War was still not over, and in a period when the views of Earl Browder were in full force. Browder, the general secretary of the Communist Party of the United States, proposed conciliation with the capitalist class and with North American imperialism in Latin America.*

In those years, the Nicaraguan workers' movement was basically made up of artisans, and this provided a base for anti-working-class deviations. In addition, the leadership of the Socialist Party was also of artisan origin, and not of proletarian roots as the Nicaraguan Socialist Party demagogically asserts. It was a leadership that suffered from an extremely low ideological level.

For many years, the revolutionary intellectual was a rare exception in Nicaragua. The radical and free-thinking intellectuals of the years of the U.S. armed intervention, who as a class represented a bourgeoisie that ended up capitulating, could not be replaced by intellectuals identified with the working class, for the reasons previously explained. As a result, the intellectual movement in Nicaragua came to be the monopoly of a Catholic element, who for a period even began to openly identify with fascism. In this way, the door of thought remained shut to the revolutionary movement.

The Nicaraguan Socialist Party was organized in a meeting whose objective was to proclaim support to Somoza's government. This took place on July 3, 1944, in the Managua gymnasium. To be rigorously

*Earl Browder (1891-1973) headed the Communist Party USA 1930-45. After the Nazi invasion of the USSR in June 1941 his name became identified with the policy (actually dictated by Stalin) of supporting capitalist governments that were at war with Nazi Germany. In Latin America this meant supporting governments that had Washington's support, and subordinating the workers' struggles to them.

objective, it's necessary to explain that this very grave error was not the result of simple bad faith by the leaders. We must look at the factors that brought it about.

The Marxist leadership did not possess the necessary clarity in the face of the Conservative sector's control over the anti-Somozaist opposition. It could not distinguish between the justice of the anti-Somozaist opposition and the maneuvers of the Conservative sector.

Once Somoza had used the pseudo-Marxist sector for his own benefit, he unleashed repression against the workers' movement, which, due to the comfortable conditions in which it was born, did not know how to defend itself with the necessary revolutionary firmness.

Parallel to this, the capitalist sector of the opposition (Conservative Party, Liberal opposition grouping) carried out all kinds of compromises with the Somoza regime.

Role of the Cuban people's struggle and revolutionary victories

The principal characteristic of the period from the assassination of Sandino in 1934 until the triumph of the Cuban revolution in 1959 was the interruption of the traditional armed struggle as a systematic tactic to fight the ruling regime. Another main characteristic was the almost total domination that the Conservative sector exerted over the anti-Somozaist opposition. That was the situation, lasting for twenty-five years, that preceded the new stage, which began with the armed struggle of the Cuban people and their victorious revolution.

There were a few exceptions to that long pacifistic period. But these were almost always insignificant actions by the Conservative sector, behind the backs of and against the people. In April 1954, an armed coup was foiled, which although under Conservative hegemony, involved elements that had revolutionary inclinations. The attitude of these revolutionary elements, along with the action of the patriot Rigoberto López Pérez, who gave his life in bringing Anastasio Somoza G. to justice on September 21, 1956, must be viewed as precursory events to the insurrectional stage that developed several years later.

The Cuban people's rebellion had an influence even before its victorious outcome. Thus, in October 1958, there was the guerrilla action in which the leader, the veteran Sandinista Ramón Raudales, was killed. There were a whole series of armed actions against the reactionary government of Nicaragua, including the following:

Ramón Raudales, in the mountains of Julapa, in October 1958; El Chaparral in June 1959; Manuel Díaz Sotelo, in Estelí, in August

1959; Carlos Haslam, in the mountains of Matagalpa, in the second half of 1959; Heriberto Reyes, in Yumale, in December 1959; Las Trojes and El Dorado, in early 1960; Orosí, on the southern border, in the second half of 1959; Luis Morales, on the San Juan River on the southern border, in January 1960; Poteca River on the northern border, January 1961; Bijao River, November 1962; the Coco River and Bocay River, in 1963; clash between peasants and local authorities in 1965 in the Uluse region of Matagalpa; economic actions against banks in 1966; actions in Managua, January 22, 1967; incursions in Pancasán in 1966 and 1967; economic bank action in Managua and certain revolutionary executions in some areas of the countryside in 1963; battle with the National Guard in Oaosca, Matagalpa, February 1969.

In some encounters, especially in the first months of the new stage, elements linked to the traditional capitalist parties were influential in the leadership of these actions. But in general, these efforts increasingly revealed the determination of the revolutionary sector to take up arms to win the country's liberation.

The period of gestation of the current revolutionary armed struggle has lasted almost ten years and this length of time is clearly a result of the characteristics of the revolutionary movement that have been explained.

The rise of the revolutionary armed organization

Especially in the first years of the new stage, the revolutionary leadership was obliged to take up arms with leaders who often lacked the political conviction needed to lead the struggle for national liberation. As the process has developed, these leaders have been replaced by comrades who possess a profound conviction and an unbreakable determination to defend the people arms in hand.

Another very prominent aspect of the first period of the new stage was the lack of an adequate revolutionary organization linked to the broad masses of the people, and especially to the peasants. It should be noted that the composition of what could be called the revolutionary groups was primarily made up of artisans and workers with a very low political and ideological level. At that time, revolutionary militants with a university student background were an exception. Students fell in different actions, but each group as such lacked the numbers needed to enable it to play a very important part in assimilating the experiences that the individual students were acquiring. The revolutionary groups lacked cadres who had the ability to solve the difficult problems that the situation posed.

One aspect that is worth looking at regarding the work that has been done over the last decade is that no one knew how to combine underground activity with work among the popular masses. In general, importance has been given only to underground activity, although after the defeat at the Bocay River in 1963 and the Coco River between 1964 and 1966 the error was committed of interrupting insurrectional work in order to pay attention to work among the masses.

It must be pointed out that for a period of time, more precisely up to 1962, each individual armed action came from a different group. That is, they reflected the total anarchy that the insurrectional revolutionary sector suffered from. The Sandinista National Liberation Front (FSLN) marked the overcoming of that problem, providing this sector with its political and military instrument.

Between 1959 and 1962, some of the components of the FSLN retained the illusion that it was possible to accomplish a change in the pacifistic line of the leadership of the Nicaraguan Socialist Party. In the year 1962 this illusion was dissolved in practice with the establishment of the Sandinista Front as an independent grouping, although for some time to come the idea was maintained that it was possible to arrive at specific unity with the Socialist Party, something which reality has refuted.

The movement that culminated at the Coco River and the Bocay River was the first action prepared by a more or less homogeneous revolutionary group. This first attempt was like a dry run for the revolutionary sector.

This first defeat led to a position marked with a reformist streak. It is true that armed struggle was not renounced and the conviction remained that this form of struggle would decide the unfolding of the Nicaraguan revolution. But the reality was that for some time the practical work of continuing the preparations for armed struggle was interrupted. It is also true that after the 1963 defeat our movement was seriously splintered, but we did not know how to adequately overcome the internal crisis that developed.

One factor that undoubtedly influenced the deviation was that our armed defeat coincided with a downturn in the anti-Somoza movement in Nicaragua. In 1963, the political ascent initiated by the struggle and victory of the Cuban people was interrupted. The basis for the downturn was that in February 1963 the Somozaist clique successfully carried out the maneuver of holding an electoral farce to impose the puppet René Schick.

In any case, although this downturn in the general situation took place, the FSLN leadership did not fully understand this to be no more than a partial phenomenon, inasmuch as the direction of the revolutionary movement was fundamentally toward progress and in transition toward maturity.

It was correct in that period to pass over to rebuilding the insurrectional organization and accumulating new forces with which to relaunch the armed struggle, but this goal naturally demanded an uninterrupted maintenance of a series of insurrectional-type tasks: accumulating material resources, training combatants, carrying out certain armed actions appropriate to the strategic defensive stage, etc.

This deviation in tactics was also expressed in the ideology that the Sandinista Front adopted. Although it raised the banner of anti-imperialism and the emancipation of the exploited classes, the Front vacillated in putting forward a clearly Marxist-Leninist ideology. The attitude that the traditional Marxist-Leninist sector had maintained in the Nicaraguan people's struggle contributed to this vacillation. As has been stated, this sector in practice has openly played the game of the Somozaist clique. This factor, together with the ideological backwardness prevailing in the revolutionary sector of the country, led to vacillation in adopting an ideology that on the national level was rooted in compromise. It can be said that at that time there was a lack of clear understanding that it was only a question of time before the youth and people of Nicaragua would begin to distinguish between the false Marxists and the true Marxists.

Consequently, in the years 1964 and 1965, practically all the emphasis was put on open work, which included legal work among the masses. Clandestine tasks were carried out, above all in the countryside, but the main emphasis of the work during that time was legal. Reality showed that legal work carried out in that manner did not serve to accumulate forces and that the progress achieved was minimal. Neither can it be overlooked that the legal work through the now-disappeared Republican Mobilization group, the student movement, and peasant movement suffered from lack of discipline, audacity, and organization.

One must also conclude that revolutionary work (whether it be public, legal, or clandestine), cannot be advanced in an accelerated way if the armed revolutionary force is lacking. It was the lack of such a force that determined the extreme limitations of the legal work carried out in the years 1964-65.

Our experience shows that the armed revolutionary force (urban and rural) is the motor force of the revolutionary movement in Nicaragua. The armed struggle is the only thing that can inspire the revolutionary combatant in Nicaragua to carry out the tasks decided on by the revolutionary leadership, whether they be armed or of any other revolutionary character.

Parenthetically, during the years 1964 and 1965 important contact with the peasant sector was developed. Comrades of urban extraction permanently established themselves in areas situated on both ends of the northern region of the country, and made trips to learn the peasants' problems firsthand and organize the revolutionary struggle in the countryside.

It must be said, however, that full advantage was not taken of the broad contact that was established with the peasants. In the countryside, some mass peasant meetings were held, some peasant delegations were sent to the city to expose the problems of the countryside, and the peasants occupied some lands, challenging the violence of the big landlords. However, an accelerated pace of peasant mobilization was not maintained. Contact was preserved at specific points and was not extended to other places where the peasants suffered terrible living and working conditions. In addition, if the few peasant marches to the city had been organized with more audacious methods, a much larger number of peasants would have participated, and at the same time a greater number of areas would have gone into action.

In various places, individual contact with certain peasants was prolonged for too long a time without proceeding to the mobilization of the peasant masses. Land invasions by the peasants who had been dispossessed were hardly ever carried out.

The lack of both adequately developed leading cadres and the necessary determination to organize the struggle of the popular masses played a decisive role in the fact that we did not fully utilize the possibilities that were presented. Lacking guerrilla camps, it was impossible to train cadres to organize the struggle of the diverse sectors of the Nicaraguan people.

The armed movement of Pancasán

In the course of 1966, practical steps were taken to relaunch armed actions. That year the Sandinista Front became conscious of the deviation that had occurred as a result of the blows of 1963 and it proceeded to prepare the Pancasán guerrilla base. Although this preparation showed organizational progress compared with the FSLN's armed movement in 1963, it did not represent serious progress in political and military tactics. It was a notable step forward organizationally because it did not follow the usual practice of preparing the armed movement in a neighboring country, which had provided distance from the enemy's observation; rather it was preparation of an armed movement in mountains situated in the very center of the country.

An extremely important factor that hindered the success of the Pancasán movement was the mistaken method used to get the peasants to participate in the struggle. The form used was to recruit a number of peasants to become part of the regular column. This means that these peasants were completely mixed in with the working-class and student fighters, i.e., combatants with an urban background.

The militants who came from urban areas generally possessed a higher revolutionary consciousness than the peasants as a whole, who became demoralized when faced with the first difficulties that we ran up against: scarcity of supplies, certain slow marches, and the first rumors of the presence of enemy soldiers on nearby roads. This obligated the leadership to send back the majority of the peasants, although there were honorable exceptions of peasants who firmly refused to be let go and who are an example of the combative possibility of this sector.

In addition, in the first stage of the revolutionary war that was beginning, we did not find a way to incorporate the peasants in those areas some days distant, with whom contact had previously been established through organizing them in the struggle for land and for other demands. Some of the peasants who temporarily joined the guerrillas had been moved from their areas to the encampments.

When the break-up of the Pancasán guerrilla movement had already taken place, it became known that once some of the peasants who had deserted the guerrillas arrived back in their own areas, they took part in armed assaults on local government posts or rural commercial establishments, as well as executions of known informers. This indicates that to a large extent some of the peasants who had become demoralized went through that crisis because they were not organized in the most appropriate manner. It means that they probably should have been irregular rather than regular guerrillas. This experience leads us to think about the possibility of organizing irregular guerrillas parallel to the regulars. We should not fail to point out that we can now evaluate the importance of work among the peasants much better, thanks to our own experience. We don't only base ourselves on the experiences of other Latin American guerrilla movements.

Another aspect that must be highlighted was the insufficient number of cadres to handle all the tasks that the preparation of the work demanded, not only in the city and the countryside, but even outside of the country. For too long the leadership of the Sandinista Front tolerated sectarianism, which stood in the way of promoting a sufficient quantity of new cadres coming from politically advanced working-class backgrounds and from the university sector. Feverish attempts were made to achieve excessively big goals instead of always making progress in carrying out suitable, everyday tasks.

The insurrectionary work was not related to the general people's struggle — especially the peasant, student, working-class struggles. It was good that the Front put its principal emphasis on insurrectionary work, but it was an error to abandon other revolutionary forms of struggle. Sectarian tactics weighed heavily and these determined the course of activity in the preparation for the movement in the mountains.

The individualistic bad habits that leadership comrades often displayed was the factor that helped hold back the initiatives that could have resolved many problems; on different occasions individual problems were mixed with political problems. This may have decisively contributed to depriving certain initiatives of the seriousness that was due them.

In regard to placing cadres in charge of various tasks, it was a mistake to be confident that comrades who had not experienced the privations of guerrilla life would be able to work among the masses — for example, among the student masses. For some years now, our organization has been conscious of the ballast that the Nicaraguan revolutionary movement carries as a result of the stance of the capitalist parties, which for many years usurped the leadership of the anti-Somozaist opposition. However, at the time when the guerrilla base was established in the mountains, there was insufficient thought given to the fact that due to the prevailing conditions the tasks required by the work in the cities could not be attended to by militants who did not possess the necessary firmness and discipline. In view of this, the comrades in the forefront of urban resistance work could count on the practical collaboration of a very reduced number of militants. The situation of the urban resistance became more acute due to the sectarian attitude of those charged with this responsibility.

Organized mass work (student, peasant, worker) was paralyzed. On the one hand, there were not enough cadres to handle this work, and on the other, there was an underestimation of the importance this activity could play in the development of the armed struggle. This weakness led to the situation where when the death of comrades in the mountains and in the cities was recorded, there was not consistent solidarity on the part of all the members of the Front.

In the cities, only violent actions of an individual nature were planned. And there was no attempt to develop a policy of using violence involving the participation of the popular masses in the cities — something that is possible mainly in Managua, the country's capital, which has a population of more than 300,000.

Under Nicaraguan conditions, as well as in most countries of Latin America, the center of action of the revolutionary war has to be the countryside. However, the cities must also play a role of particular importance, given that in the first stage of the war the city has to supply the countryside with the most developed cadres to lead the political and military detachment. In general, the revolutionary elements from the cities have a greater ability to develop themselves in the first stage. These elements are composed of the revolutionary sector of workers, students, and a certain layer of the petty bourgeoisie.

One must take into account the habits that the capitalist parties and their faithful servants have imposed on the popular masses through their electoral policy. These parties have conditioned broad sectors of the people to participate in the hustle and bustle of electoral rigamarole. This circumstance must be taken into account to fully understand why many sectors of the population, despite their sympathy with the revolutionary armed struggle, cannot demonstrate that sympathy through action. This forces us to consider the need to fully train a broad number of persons from among the population to have the material capacity to support the armed struggle. To seek out the people is not sufficient; they have to be trained to participate in the revolutionary war.

Some current tasks

Several months ago, work in the countryside was reestablished. The FSLN is simultaneously developing political and military work, with the objective of reorganizing the guerrilla struggle.

In the countryside a study of the peasants' problems is already under way, and this investigation has required militants to stay in the rural zones for several weeks. Militants with an urban background (workers and students) are participating in this political work. It has been said that the mountain (the guerrilla base) proletarianizes, and we agree with this statement. But as our experience has shown, it can be added that the countryside — political contact with the peasants — also proletarianizes. The urban militant, in contact with the countryside, including the zones where a guerrilla base is not organized, lives the abject poverty that the peasants suffer and feels their desire to struggle.

A phenomenon that has been seen in this country since the Pancasán movement is the growth of the Sandinista National Liberation Front's political authority over the broad sectors of the popular masses. Today the Sandinista Front can claim, and has obtained, a much greater degree of cooperation from the population than in the past. It must also be said that if we do not get greater cooperation than we actually are receiving, it is because we lack cadres who are competent in asking for this type of help, and also because the cadres now active are not functioning systematically enough.

Simultaneously, new methods are being found so that we can gain the practical collaboration of new sectors of the population in the clandestine conditions under which we function (a small country with small cities). This has led us to not depend exclusively on the old militants and collaborators (a large proportion of whom are "jaded").

Furthermore, we have reestablished squads that are prepared to act in the cities, and they have carried out some actions.

We now have plans to undertake actions in harmony with the period of reestablishment we are now going through.

The Sandinista National Liberation Front believes that at the present time and for a certain period to come, Nicaragua will be going through a stage in which a radical political force will be developing its specific characteristics. Consequently, at the current time it is necessary for us to strongly emphasize that our major objective is the socialist revolution, a revolution that aims to defeat Yankee imperialism and its local agents, false oppositionists, and false revolutionaries. This propaganda, with the firm backing of armed action, will permit the Front to win the support of a sector of the popular masses that is conscious of the profound nature of the struggle we are carrying out.

In order to outline a strategy for the revolutionary movement, it is necessary to take into account the strength that the capitalist parties represent, due to the influence they still wield within the opposition. One must be alert to the danger that the reactionary force in the opposition to the Somoza regime could climb on the back of the revolutionary insurrection. The revolutionary movement has a dual goal. On the one hand, to overthrow the criminal and traitorous clique that has usurped the power for so many years; and on the other, to prevent the capitalist opposition — of proven submission to Yankee imperialism — from taking advantage of the situation which the guerrilla struggle has unleashed, and grabbing power. In the task of barring the way to the traitorous capitalist forces, a revolutionary political and military force rooted in the broad sectors of the people has a unique role to play. Sinking these roots is dependent on the organization's ability to drive out the Liberal and Conservative influences from this broad sector.

The policy we follow later on regarding the old parties that now have a capitalist leadership will be determined by the attitude that the people as a whole have toward these parties.

Relating to the situation of the Nicaraguan Socialist Party, it can be stated that the changes that have taken place in that political organization's leadership are purely changes in form. The old leadership builds illusions regarding the Conservative sector, and calls for building a political front in which these stubborn agents of imperialism participate. The so-called new leadership currently justifies having participated in the electoral farce of 1967, supporting the pseudo-oppositional candidacy of the Conservative politician Fernando Aguero. Like the old leadership, the so-called new leadership keeps talking about the armed struggle, while in practice it concentrates its energies on petty legal work.

The above statements do not contradict the possibility of developing a certain unity with the anti-Somozaist sector in general. But this is unity at the base, with the most honest sectors of the various anti-Somozaist tendencies. This is all the more possible due to the increase in the prestige of the Sandinista National Liberation Front and the discrediting and splintering of the leadership of the capitalist parties and the like.

The Sandinista National Liberation Front understands how hard the guerrilla road is. But it is not prepared to retreat. We know that we are confronting a bloody, reactionary armed force like the National Guard, the ferocious GN, which maintains intact the practices of cruelty that were inculcated in it by its creator, the U.S. Marines. Bombardment of villages, cutting of children's throats, violation of women, burning huts with peasants inside of them, mutilation as a torture — these were the study courses that the U.S. professors of civilization taught the GN during the period of the guerrilla resistance (1927-1932) led by Augusto César Sandino.

The frustration that followed the period of the Sandinista resistance does not have to be repeated today. Now the times are different. The current days are not like those in which Sandino and his guerrilla brothers battled alone against the Yankee empire. Today revolutionaries of all the subjugated countries are rising up or preparing to go into the battle against the empire of the dollar. At the apex of this battle is indominatable Vietnam, which with its example of heroism, is repulsing the aggression of the blond beasts.

The combative example of our fallen brothers carries us forward. It is the example of Casimiro Sotelo, Danilo Rosales, Jorge Navarro, Francisco Buitrago, Silvio Mayorga, Otto Casco, Modesto Duarte, Robert Amaya, Edmundo Pérez, Hugo Medina, René Carrión, Rigoberto Cruz (Pablo Ubeda), Fermín Díaz, Selín Chible, Ernesto Fernández, Oscar Florez, Felipe Gaitán, Fausto García, Elías Moncada, Francisco Moreno, Carlos Reyna, David Tejada, Carlos Tinoco, Francisco Córdoba, Faustino Ruíz, Boanerges Santamaría, Iván Sánchez.

We will faithfully fulfill our oath:

"Before the image of Augusto César Sandino and Ernesto Che Guevara; before the memory of the heroes and martyrs of Nicaragua, Latin America, and humanity as a whole; before history: I place my hand on the black and red flag that signifies 'Free Homeland or Death,' and I swear to defend the national honor with arms in hand and to fight for the redemption of the oppressed and exploited in Nicaragua and the world. If I fulfill this oath, the freedom of Nicaragua and all the peoples will be the reward; if I betray this oath, death in disgrace and dishonor will be my punishment."

Nothing Will Hold Back Our Struggle for Liberation

by Daniel Ortega

This speech by FSLN leader Daniel Ortega was delivered to the plenary session of the Sixth Summit Conference of Nonaligned Countries held in Havana September 3-9, 1979. Ortega is coordinator of Nicaragua's Junta of National Reconstruction. The translation is by Intercontinental Press.

In January 1928 the Panamerican Conference was held in Havana. At that time the Nicaraguan people were engaged in an unequal struggle against Yankee intervention. Calvin Coolidge, who was then president of the United States, participated in the Havana meeting, and the tyrant Machado was president of Cuba.

Sandino, hoping to gain the support of some delegations, sent the following message on January 2, 1928:

> Our voices must be heard in Havana. Men must not lack the moral courage to speak the truth about our misfortune. They must tell how the people of Nicaragua, who are valiantly fighting and suffering, are determined to make any sacrifice, even including their own extermination, in order to defend their liberty. The results in Havana will be null and void if the ideal of the Spanish-speaking peoples is not crystallized; if you let us be assassinated to the last man, we will have the consolation of knowing that we carried out our duty. Our Country and Freedom.
>
> A. C. Sandino

Not a single voice was raised at that Havana meeting.

Today Havana is serving as the site for this Sixth Summit, and the peoples and governments that are represented in this assembly are motivated by common interests.

A free and hospitable people, filled with solidarity, is receiving these delegations. And the leader of the revolution carried out by this people is presiding over the Nonaligned for this period. The tyrant Machado no longer governs Cuba. It is the people of Cuba who determine their own destiny.

The Government of National Reconstruction of Nicaragua and the Sandinista National Liberation Front salute the people of Cuba, their government, and the president of the Council of State, Comandante and Comrade Fidel Castro.

We also salute the peoples of Latin America, the Caribbean, Africa, and Asia for the solidarity they demonstrated in support of our cause.

On Saturday, September 1, in a Mexican newspaper, we read a dispatch datelined Havana that made reference to Nicaragua's position regarding the "problem" of Kampuchea. And we say "problem" because it is a problem for imperialism for *a people to be free*.

The dispatch in question noted that Nicaragua's delegation had aligned itself with the Soviet bloc by recognizing the government of people's Kampuchea. We all know what interests motivate the international press agencies of the so-called free world, so the deed does not surprise us.

We know that many of these press agencies, and with them the most reactionary sectors of the United States government and of Latin America, are waiting to pounce on our declarations at this meeting.

These are the same forces that gave rise to the Somozaist dictatorship. They are the same forces that defamed and assassinated Lumumba,* that defamed and assassinated Che. These are the same forces that slandered and assassinated Van Troi,** the same forces that slandered and assassinated Sandino.

Imperialism cannot conceive of a free people, a sovereign people, an independent people. Because, simply and plainly, for them *the people* is nothing more than an empty phrase. We just saw reconfirmation of this when our final offensive was launched.

They examined the war in mathematical terms. Somoza had a regular army. Somoza had more soldiers than the Sandinistas. Somoza had tanks, planes, artillery, while the Sandinistas didn't. Somoza had more soldiers, more rifles, more communications than the Sandinistas. Therefore, Somoza had to win the war against the Sandinistas. But what was left out was that Somoza did not have the people, and that we Sandinistas were the people.

And when Somoza was losing the war, they were talking about Costa Rican intervention, Panamanian intervention, Cuban intervention,

---

*Patrice Lumumba, a leader of the struggle for Congolese liberation, was the first premier of the Republic of the Congo. His government was overthrown by a military coup involving the CIA, and he was murdered in 1961.

**Nguyen Van Troi was a Vietnamese freedom fighter.

Soviet intervention — simply because they have never been able to understand, and are never going to understand, that people are capable of achieving their liberation, that people are able to solidarize themselves with people, and that therefore the free and sovereign people of Nicaragua today recognizes the right of Kampuchea to occupy this seat.

I repeat, imperialism cannot understand it because for them *the people* is nothing more than an empty phrase.

The Nicaraguan people have won, with their blood, the right to be here today, in this way breaking with a historic past of servility toward imperialist policy.

For the first time in their entire history the Nicaraguan people can officially express their sovereign will, joining this movement of the Nonaligned barely forty-one days after their triumph.

We are entering the Nonaligned movement because in this movement we see the broadest organization of the Third World states that are playing an important role and exercising a growing influence in the international sphere, in the struggle of peoples against imperialism, colonialism, neocolonialism, apartheid, racism, including Zionism and every form of oppression. Because they are for active peaceful coexistence, against the existence of military blocs and alliances, for restructuring international relations on an honorable basis, and are for the establishment of a new international economic order.

In the Sandinista revolution there is no alignment; there is an absolute and consistent commitment to the aspirations of the peoples who have achieved their independence and to those who are struggling to win it. That is why we are among the Nonaligned.

This transcendental step is part of the process of liberation that peoples are going through, peoples such as those in Grenada, Iran, Kampuchea, and Uganda, who won beautiful victories this year.

In 1855 a certain William Walker arrived from the southern slave states of the United States with a gang of mercenaries, to make himself master of our country and of all of Central America.

The individual in question named himself president of Nicaragua and his first decree was the reestablishment of slavery; the United States press and more than a few U.S. legislators made William Walker into a hero.

In September 1856, after continual and bloody resistance, the people of Nicaragua and the peoples of Central America defeated the invader, who was obliged to flee to his country of origin, where he was received as a hero.

Some months later he again tried to invade our country. During his third attempt he was captured in Honduras, a country bordering on Nicaragua, and was shot. In 1909 a Liberal president named José Santos Zelaya, who tried to open new markets in Europe, was forced to resign by a note sent by the U.S. secretary of state of that time. But what Señor Zelaya lacked, the Nicaraguan people had plenty of, and they rose up against Yankee intervention.

Because we reject Yankee intervention we are in the Nonaligned. For that reason, and because we are Sandinistas, we demand the reintegration, the unconditional return of the Guantánamo base to Cuba, and we recognize the heroic and unequal struggle waged by the Cuban people against the criminal blockade.

That is why we support the struggle of the people of Puerto Rico for self-determination and independence, and why we are in solidarity with Lolita Lebrón and her companions in prison,* who are authentic representatives of the struggle of the people of Puerto Rico.

That is why we stand behind the people of Panama in their struggle for sovereignty over the Canal Zone.

That is why we are with the people of Belize in their struggle for independence, for self-determination, and for territorial integrity.

Regular troops of the Yankee marines landed in our country in 1910 in an attempt to suppress our people's desire for independence. Bloody struggles were unleashed and this armed intervention was maintained until 1926, the year they withdrew, believing the situation to be under control.

Because we are Sandinistas and because just causes are our causes, we have, from the beginning, identified with the struggle of the heroic people of Vietnam, and we condemn all the aggressions that have taken place and are taking place against the people and government of Vietnam, which fought, and is fighting, against aggression and foreign occupation.

We also support the just struggle of the people of Western Sahara, and from this moment Nicaragua must be included among the countries that fully recognize the Democratic Arab Sahraoui Republic and the Polisario Front as the only and the legitimate representative of the heroic people of Western Sahara.

That is why we recognize the legitimate rights of the people of Namibia, represented by SWAPO. We support the Patriotic Front of Zimbabwe, the sole representative of this people, and we condemn the im-

---

*Lolita Lebrón was one of five Puerto Rican nationalists imprisoned in the U.S. in the early 1950s for armed proindependence actions. She and the three other surviving prisoners were released in 1979.

perialist maneuvers in Rhodesia, the puppet regime of Muzorewa, and the so-called internal settlement.*

We solidarize ourselves with the frontline countries and condemn the aggression by South Africa and Rhodesia against them. And we solidarize with the right of the people of East Timor to self-determination.

We support the reunification of Korea and we demand the withdrawal of U.S. troops from South Korea.

Only a few months were to pass when in 1927 Yankee marines again landed on our soil.

Then the figure of Augusto César Sandino vigorously rose up and, at the head of an army of workers and peasants, sought to militarily defeat the interventionist forces in an unequal campaign.

Sandino embodied the desire for liberty of a people who were systematically subjected to the attack of Yankee intervention and subjected to imperialist exploitation and domination. The same marines who murdered the Filipino people thousands of miles from our country, arrived to soak Nicaraguan territory in blood in those days.

This explains the existence of Sandinismo, which on May 4, 1927, gave rise to what Sandino called the "war of liberators to end the war of the oppressors."

The Yankees, who were unable to defeat Sandino's army militarily, who found themselves forced to withdraw in January 1932, again resorted to treachery, using as their instrument an army and an army chief named Anastasio Somoza García, founder of the dynasty. This army and this army chief were created by the White House strategists to assassinate Sandino.

They thought that killing Sandino would solve the problem. They did not take into account that Sandino had initiated a process of liberation which, carried on by the Sandinista National Liberation Front, was to win one of its most important victories on July 19, 1979. On that day we both defeated the criminal Somozaist National Guard and expelled the last Yankee marine, Anastasio Somoza, from Nicaragua.

Our country is a small country, a poor country.

---

*The internal settlement was a plan imposed by the white minority regime in Rhodesia (Zimbabwe) to institute nominal Black rule while maintaining the economic and political structure of white domination. Abel Muzorewa, a Black clergyman, was installed as prime minister under this set-up in June 1979. Lacking support from the Black majority, the plan collapsed, and, after elections in March 1980, Robert Mugabe of the Patriotic Front became prime minister.

A little more than 2.5 million Nicaraguans live in 128,000 square kilometers. It is a country that is basically dependent on agriculture, and its production was paralyzed by the war. A country that had few factories, which were destroyed by the Somoza air force.

A country with a small population that has had to sacrifice thousands of its best children to repel three armed Yankee interventions that have left more than 200,000 victims. A country that in its final offensive against the Somozaist dictatorship suffered more than 50,000 deaths, a high percentage of whom, 90 percent of the total, were youth from eight years of age to twenty.

A country with its schools and hospitals destroyed, with its cities leveled by 500-pound bombs given to Somoza by the United States and Israeli Zionism. But we were not alone in the struggle. We know that we had the backing of the peoples of the world. We know that this was what made it impossible for the Yankees to carry out a new armed intervention in our country before the tyrant was destroyed.

Among the files abandoned by Somozaism we have found proof of the loans for arms that the government of Israel had given to the dictatorship. Israel was an accomplice to the crimes of Somoza. Israel was the instrument that imperialism used up to the last moment to arm Somoza's genocidal dictatorship. Rockets, rifles, howitzers, planes, gunboats, and even helmets and uniforms were sent to the dictator. But the strength of the people was greater than that of the aggression.

As we said at that time, we will not repay these loans, this debt that adds up to millions of dollars. Nor will we pay any debt contracted with other countries for armaments for the Somozaist regime. On the contrary, it is Israel that owes a debt to our people.

We are Sandinistas; our people have been struggling against oppression and interventions for more than 150 years. That is why we have historically identified with the struggle of the Palestinian people and we recognize the PLO as their legitimate representative. And that is why we condemn Israeli occupation of the Arab territories and demand their unconditional return.

We support genuine efforts in the search for a just and true peace in the Middle East. But such a peace must take into account the interests of all the parties, and in the first place the rights of the Palestinian people.

On May 4, 1927, at the moment Sandino was rising up, a Nicaraguan traitor signed away the sovereignty of the people of Nicaragua to the Yankee government, in exchange for a dollar for each rifle turned in. We condemn the Camp David accords, which, like the shameful treason of 1927 in Nicaragua, merit our energetic repudiation.

In June 1979, there were forces in the U.S. government that wanted to propose an invasion of our soil to the seventeenth meeting of representatives of the Organization of American States. But there were also seventeen Latin American countries that said no to the imperialist proposal.

Here we must make special mention and take recognition of the Andean Pact countries.

We should mention the names of President Rodrigo Carazo of Costa Rica; ex-President Carlos Andrés Pérez of Venezuela; President José López Portillo of Mexico; General Omar Torrijos of Panama; and Fidel Castro of Cuba — all of whom were and continue to be in solidarity with our struggle, despite the risks that such solidarity implies.

We should make special mention of the militant solidarity that Latin American fighters gave our struggle. The blood of these fighters was shed along the road to victory. We can state that Latin America helped to make this victory possible.

We are a small country that has waged war in order to win peace. And we support the establishment of a just and lasting peace that extends to all countries and regions.

We recognize the right of peoples to win their freedom through the path that is best for them, whether armed or not.

We are a poor country that wants to take the efforts and resources now being invested in defense of the revolution and invest it in tractors and plows. And we support general and complete disarmament, under strict international control. We are for an end to the arms race and we salute the SALT II accords as an important step in this direction. We demand respect for the territorial integrity of states and renunciation of the use of force in international relations. We condemn the existence of military bases.

Sandinismo is the incarnation of the nation. The Sandinista National Liberation Front, as the genuine vanguard of the great people's insurrection that defeated the dictatorship, is now pushing forward a process of national reconstruction whose first measures have been the massive expropriation of the property of Somoza and his civilian and military accomplices. So far more than 500,000 hectares, close to 50 percent of the entire arable area of the country, has been recovered by the people.

More than 180 industrial and commercial enterprises have passed into the hands of the people.

More than 400 mansions and homes have been expropriated in the interests of the people.

The banks have been nationalized.

We have begun to put an Integral Agrarian Reform Plan into effect. Agricultural exports have been nationalized.

The exploitation of natural resources has been nationalized.

By eliminating the 500 and 1,000 *córdoba* bills* and retiring them from circulation, we are hindering the maneuvers of the defeated Somozaists to destabilize our country financially.

A real social thrust is being given to education, health, and housing.

A foreign policy of relations with all countries of the world has been established.

We have become part of the movement of the Nonaligned.

Sandinista Defense Committees have been organized as bodies of people's participation.

The Sandinista People's Army has been set up to fulfill the pressing need to guarantee the defense and advance of the revolution.

And this revolution has been expansive and generous toward its enemies. Thousands of captured soldiers have had their lives protected. Groups such as the International Red Cross were authorized to set up centers of refuge to give shelter to the Somozaist criminals who were fleeing.

The revolution is marching forward. The difficulties are great. The counterrevolution is a potential threat.

There are some who assert that we are assassinating the prisoners.

There are some who are trying to put conditions on international aid. The conspiracy is powerful and the most reactionary sectors of the U.S. government have already succeeeded in stopping a small grant of $8 million that the U.S. government was going to give our country.

The most reactionary sectors of the Central American region are observing our process with trepidation. We have detected concentrations of Somozaist soldiers in neighboring countries. But just as we have been generous in victory, we will be inflexible in defense of the revolution.

To what has already been described, we must add the economic legacy of imperialist domination and the Somozaist war of aggression.

We find ourselves with a foreign debt of more than $1.53 billion. Of this amount, $596 million falls due this year, having been incurred as short-term loans at very high interest rates. The foreign debt is equivalent to three times the total annual exports of the country.

The loans obtained by Somozaism were misspent, squandered, and sent out of the country to personal accounts in the United States and Europe.

*1 córdoba = US$.10

A study published August 14 by the Economic Commission for Latin America (CEPAL) maintained that Somozaist bombing resulted in $580 million in material damage to the physical and social infrastructure in the agricultural, industrial, and commercial sectors. At present $741 million is needed to reactivate production.

To the losses cited above, we have to add the losses to the system of production that stem from the paralysis of economic activities. In addition we must add the resources required for restoring the country's economic apparatus at a time when it is also being transformed.

To give us a more graphic representation of the problem, CEPAL estimates that the situation we have described means that the Gross Domestic Product has declined 25 percent this year, 1979. In per capita terms, this puts the GDP back to the level that Nicaragua was at in 1962, meaning we have slid back seventeen years.

And to top it all off, our revolution found only $3.5 million in the state coffers. That is all that Somozaism was unable to loot.

Nicaragua's situation has provoked interest in the countries of Latin America and the rest of the world. Regional bodies have expressed their decision to aid us. Bilaterally we have close relations with many countries.

But we must be frank: The oppressive financial problem that confronts our process, which is directly related to restructuring the foreign debt and receiving financing in order to allow our economy to start up again, does not seem to seriously interest the developed countries.

The government of Mexico, which has aided us to the extent it is able, has raised the idea of an international sale of solidarity bonds that would come due at a deferred period and with low interest. Through this bond issue the debt that falls due this year, which as we said totals $596 million, would be restructured on adequate terms. We support the proposal of President Didier Rasiratekat of Madagascar, regarding the creation of a Financial Fund of the Nonaligned countries.

We believe it is our duty to present before the movement of the Nonaligned both the advances and the problems of the revolution in Nicaragua.

We believe that by consolidating the Nicaraguan revolution we will be strengthening the struggle of the underdeveloped countries.

We know that imperialism is interested in seeing our process fail and that it is going to use all the resources at its disposal to achieve that.

The liberation struggle in our country is continuing. And today more than ever we need the disinterested support of the Nonaligned. Nicaragua, which forty-one days after its triumph is showing you both the open wounds and the consolidation of our revolution, is a challenge for this movement.

The people of Sandino are not going to step back from the ground already gained. Our integration with the peoples of Africa and Asia raises our morale in this great battle. The future belongs to the peoples.

The march toward victory will not be stopped!

Nicaragua — The Strategy of Victory

Interview with Humberto Ortega

Humberto Ortega is a leader of the FSLN and the commander in chief of the Sandinista People's Army. This interview, conducted by the exiled Chilean journalist Marta Harnecker, originally appeared in English in the January 27, 1980, issue of Granma. *Minor stylistic changes have been made for consistency and readability.*

Marta Harnecker: The armed struggle of the Nicaraguan people for liberation has been a long one. I have read your book *50 años de lucha sandinista* (50 Years of Sandinista Struggle) in which you described the highlights of the struggle up to 1975. However, two years ago there seemed to be little likelihood that victory would be obtained so quickly. What made possible the big gains registered by the revolutionary process which led to the overthrow of Somoza and his regime?

Humberto Ortega: Well, before I answer your question directly, I would like to briefly sum up the key points of the book you mentioned — though this is very hard to do without falling into oversimplifications and omissions.

The revolutionary movement which took shape in our country in the thirties as a result of Sandino's struggle —

Harnecker: Which took shape or began?

Ortega: Well, we say that it took shape because it summed up all previous efforts at revolutionary struggle in Nicaragua, and because Sandino assimilated the most revolutionary ideas of his time and was able to integrate them into our historical process.

He undoubtedly began it and in the course of its development he included a number of political, ideological, anti-imperialist, internationalist, and military facets. That is what we mean by the movement taking shape. That is, the struggle Sandino carried out against the Yankees for seven years left us with a number of historical and programmatic elements and revolutionary views which we assimilated.

We must bear in mind that, if we include Sandino's movement, by that time there had already been thirty-three armed movements against imperialism and the oligarchy, headed by the Liberals who upheld revolutionary positions in that period.

The struggle Sandino led suffered a bitter setback as a result of his death and that of other members of his general staff. However, in one way or another, the people always reacted against the oppression. The reaction was poor, limited, and fragmented, but it increased little by little.

The most significant upsurge in these struggles took place in the fifties, the decade when Anastasio Somoza García, founder of the tyranny, was executed by Rigoberto López Pérez.* It was an individual action but it was not simply a case of tyrannicide. As Pérez himself put it, it turned out to be "the beginning of the end of the tyranny."

Then, in 1958, while Fidel was in the Sierra Maestra, an armed movement led by Ramón Raudales began, and the following year it was the guerrilla group led by Carlos Fonseca. From 1958 to 1961 there were nineteen armed movements that sought to do battle against the dictatorship.

The victory of the Cuban revolution caused a tremendous political upheaval. It made a big impact on our people, who witnessed a practical example of how it was possible to overthrow a tyrant.

The 1959-60 period was one in which conditions were created to set up a revolutionary vanguard that could lead the popular and revolutionary war in the same way and with the same effectiveness as Sandino.

In 1961 the Sandinista Front emerged from several armed groups as an alternative to the forces that at that time led the struggle against Somoza, the so-called historical parallels or Liberal-Conservative forces.

The Sandinista Front was a new alternative, but at the same time it followed up on the legacy of the revolutionary movement Sandino started.

After it was founded there was a long period in which, in addition to very important organizational and military experience which was of great value for the future of the movement, the FSLN acquired moral standing, dedication, tenacity, and set an example which made it possible to reach out to the masses, organize them, and win their confidence. During that period, the repression of the regime was focused on the guerrillas.

*In 1956, the poet Rigoberto López Pérez walked into a public affair for Somoza in the city of León and shot the dictator four times. Somoza later died from his wounds, and López Pérez was killed on the spot by the dictator's bodyguards.

The most important operation carried out by the Front to make itself known to the world was undertaken on December 27, 1974, when a house full of top officials of the regime was taken over.* We obtained a million dollars, for the first time the Sandinistas' revolutionary views were broadcast on TV and radio, and political prisoners were rescued.

The main objective of this rather isolated operation was not achieved: to strengthen the guerrillas in the mountains. Somoza unleashed a tremendous repressive campaign in the cities, the countryside, and the mountains, where the movement was trying to set up guerrilla forces that were in the stage of making contacts and setting up their columns. From 1974 to 1977 thousands of people were killed and thousands of others disappeared.

That repression combined with our weakness prevented the guerrillas from going on the offensive. We were unable to channel the political potential and capitalize on the agitation resulting from the Sandinista operation. That made it possible for the enemy to deprive us of the initiative, and press censorship, a state of siege, martial law, and courts-martial were all imposed.

This period of relative stagnation ended in October 1977, when a Sandinista offensive began with the capture of the National Guard garrison at San Carlos, near the border with Costa Rica, on the thirteenth, and it continued with the attack and capture of the town of Mozonte, five kilometers from Ocotal, in the department of Nueva Segovia, on the fifteenth. The guerrillas held a meeting in the public square of Mozonte before withdrawing. Two days later there was an attack on the main garrison in Masaya, less than twenty kilometers from the capital, and there was an important ambush of enemy forces on the move. For over four hours, four comrades managed to contain all the enemy forces coming from Managua to Masaya. On the twenty-fifth, three squads from an FSLN column took the town of San Fernando, and the soldiers stationed there surrendered.

These developments paved the way for a qualitative change in the political and military picture. That's when our flexible policy of allian-

---

*On December 27, 1974, eight FSLN guerrillas seized the home of a former minister of agriculture during a party and took hostage thirty top Somozaist officials. They succeeded in obtaining the release of more than a dozen of their imprisoned comrades and a ransom of more than a million dollars. On December 30, the guerrillas freed the last of their hostages and fled to Cuba along with the freed prisoners.

ces began, and from it emerged the Group of Twelve.*

Harnecker: But what made possible the events of October 1977?

Ortega: October 1977 came about thanks to an offensive shift that was given to the armed struggle at a time when the crisis of Somoza's regime was very acute.

Following the 1972 earthquake, the situation of Somoza's regime became more acute and bureaucratic and military corruption more widespread. While this administrative corruption chiefly affected the masses, it also began to affect the petty and intermediate bourgeoisie, thus increasing the scope of opposition to the regime.

On the other hand, groups of businessmen started to lose faith in the dictatorship's ability to guarantee the necessary conditions for the development of the country. There was growing internal resistance from all segments of the population, in addition to the growing opposition internationally due to the regime's repressive policy.

While Somoza lost more and more political and moral authority, we gained it, in spite of the difficult conditions facing our tenacious guerrillas in the northern mountains, where the forces of the Pablo Ubeda column were striving to regain the initiative, which the dictatorship had for all practical purposes deprived us of by late 1975.

This tenacious effort in addition to the daily antlike tactics of our members all over the country made it possible for our movement, far from being wiped out, to remain in action even under those difficult conditions. If this had not been accomplished, it wouldn't have been possible later on to transform the political and moral potential into military power, into a large force, as happened.

The acute economic crisis and the growing resistance of the people led to a political crisis in the country. Business groups which until then had adjusted their interests to the terms imposed by the dictatorship shifted to a position of overt opposition. A group of members of the Conservative Party led by the editor of *La Prensa*, Pedro Joaquín Chamorro, joined the Democratic Union of Liberation (UDEL), an anti-Somoza opposition organization led by dissatisfied sectors of the bourgeoisie. UDEL demanded political and trade union freedoms; an end to the press censorship, the state of siege, and the repression; and called for amnesty and a general pardon for political prisoners and exiles.

In mid-1977 there was great political activity among the bourgeois

---

*The "Group of Twelve" was a bloc of intellectuals, professionals, and businessmen who came together in late 1977 to oppose the Somoza dictatorship and to call for FSLN participation in any post-Somoza government.

opposition resulting from the shift given to U.S. foreign policy by the Carter administration.

Imperialism and reaction were seeking ways of making changes in the regime without touching the basic strings of power: the tremendous economic and repressive power of the National Guard.

The political situation forced Somoza to try to improve his image. On September 19 the state of siege and martial law were lifted, and the dictator convened municipal elections.

We must keep in mind that these efforts at democratization or overhauling took place in 1977, when imperialism and reaction were convinced that they had been able to wipe out or practically wipe out the FSLN.

From 1975 to 1977, they had played all their cards to try to crush us militarily. In order to do so they devastated vast portions of the countryside, repression was stepped up in the cities, and courts-martial were instituted. Nearly all our leaders, Carlos Fonseca, Eduardo Contreras, Carlos Agüero, Edgar Munguía, and Filemón Rivero, had been killed.

It was very diffcult for the FSLN to mount a military response and that response was very limited.

Somoza and the Yankees swore that they had eliminated us and, therefore, that we would be unable to serve as the catalyst for the crisis. When they felt that we were hard hit, scattered and divided, they decided it was time for a democratization plan.

It was at that time and in order to prevent such maneuvers that we decided to go on the offensive militarily speaking.

We regained the initiative which we had taken on December 27, 1974, but this time we aimed to avoid losing it again. We didn't have a big mass organization, but we did have our activists and the organizational potential which little by little allowed us to organize and mobilize the masses. We didn't have superior forms of organization of the vanguard, but we did realize that, given the situation, military action would allow us to make our presence felt in the political and organizational fields, paving the way for the establishment of an insurrectional strategy.

Harnecker: How could you have decided on an offensive if the Front was in such a precarious situation?

Ortega: It's true that we were in a precarious situation and that in spite of our efforts we were unable to stay on the military offensive. In practice we were on the defensive, and we had to try to overcome that situation while avoiding the twin pitfalls of adventurism and an overly conservative analysis of this difficult and precarious situation.

In order to undertake offensive operations we had to overcome a certain conservative frame of mind which led our movement to passively accumulate forces. When I say "passive," I mean in general, not in particular, because there were operations in which we regained the initiative militarily speaking.

Harnecker: Could you explain further what you mean by passive accumulation of forces?

Ortega: What I mean by passive accumulation of forces is a policy of not getting involved in the conjunctures, of gaining strength while standing on the sidelines; a passive policy of alliances. It's a passive view which holds that it is possible to pile up weapons and gain in organization and number without fighting the enemy, while sitting on the sidelines, without involving the masses — not because we didn't want to do so but because we felt that if we showed our claws too much, they would come down hard on us and shatter the movement.

We knew we would be going on the offensive under difficult circumstances, but we knew we had the necessary minimum of resources to tackle this new stage.

By May 1977 we had drawn up a programmatic platform which outlined an insurrectional strategy that served to sum up the strategic viewpoint of insurrection which I, along with Carlos Fonseca, had prepared in 1975. This was in turn an outgrowth of the efforts made along these lines after the death of Oscar Turcios and Ricardo Morales in September 1973, following the Chilean coup. This marked the start of the debate within our ranks over the two strategies: guerrilla warfare centered in the mountains, on the one hand, and armed struggle focused on the masses, on the other.

That was the first debate. It was a bit immature and categorical: it's either the mountains or the cities. Raising this question as one or the other was not correct.

Harnecker: I'd like to know why you associate the masses with the cities and not with the guerrillas.

Ortega: The truth is that we always took the masses into account, but more in terms of their supporting the guerrillas, so that the guerrillas as such could defeat the National Guard. This isn't what actually happened. What happened was that it was the guerrillas who provided support for the masses so that they could defeat the enemy by means of insurrection. We all held that view, and it was practice that showed that in order to win we had to mobilize the masses and get them to actively participate in the armed struggle. The guerrillas alone weren't enough, because the armed movement of the vanguard would never have had the weapons needed to defeat the enemy. Only in theory could we obtain the weapons and resources needed to defeat the National Guard. We realized that our chief source of strength lay in maintaining a state of total mobilization that would disperse the technical and military resources of the enemy.

Since production, the highways, and the social order in general were affected, the enemy was unable to move his forces and other means about at will because he had to cope with mass mobilizations, neighborhood demonstrations, barricades, acts of sabotage, etc. This enabled the vanguard, which was reorganizing its army, to confront the more numerous enemy forces on a better footing.

Getting back to what I was saying: the reactionaries were planning to cope with the crisis and come out on top. We realized what was happening, took note of the fact that the enemy had taken a step forward by lifting the state of siege and was considering an amnesty, and saw that if this happened we would be in a difficult position. So we decided to speed up the offensive.

Harnecker: An offensive which, as far as you are concerned, was limited.

Ortega: Well, since we had never experienced an insurrection, we felt that that was the way to mobilize the masses to support those operations. But practice showed us that we were still unable to meet all the conditions required for a response by the masses so that the drive would take on an insurrectional character. Two years had to pass before this was accomplished.

This offensive took place as part of an insurrectional strategy, but it was not an insurrection although we called for one. As it turned out, these operations served as propaganda for insurrection.

Harnecker: Did you consider what failure would have meant?

Ortega: Yes, we did. If we failed it would be a terrible blow for Sandinismo. We had to run the risk. We knew we wouldn't be wiped out because we knew our enemy. Of course, there was always a risk, but being wiped out without going on the offensive was worse than being wiped out on the offensive, because by fighting we could begin a process leading to victory. If we didn't take the political and military offensive, defeat was certain. That was the problem we faced.

Harnecker: Then you don't feel the October operations were a failure even though the insurrection didn't come about?

Ortega: We view October as a historic achievement, because, first of all, it enabled us to defeat the imperialist scheme. When the enemy felt that we had been destroyed, we appeared on the scene stronger than ever, we struck harder blows than ever before. They were surprised when we began operations in the cities, because they thought the cities were sacred.

On the other hand, although there was a crisis, the masses did not react to it. All they could see was that the vanguard was being hit hard. These operations served to restore Sandinismo's hegemony over the masses and the confidence of the masses in their economic and political struggles. This led the regime to make serious mistakes, the biggest one being murdering Pedro Joaquín Chamorro on January 10, 1978.

This assassination led the masses to take to the streets for the first time, to express their long pent-up feelings of support for Sandinismo. So we can say that October served to deepen the crisis which imperialism and reaction were on the brink of turning to their own advantage.

Harnecker: When did you start preparing for the October operations?

Ortega: Even before May 1977 we were acquiring weapons and laying the political and strategic groundwork, like the programmatic platform I mentioned, trying to see how we could organize the people who shared our views.

We reacted to the situation with what we had, given the situation. We had been stockpiling, stockpiling for something bigger, but you can't stockpile on the sidelines because then you never really stockpile.

We plunged into the offensive realizing that our effort would bear fruit because we took note of the prevailing crisis, the enemy plots, the fact that we were on the defensive and had to respond then and there. Had we been conservative and said "No, we'll stockpile in silence," we would have lost our chance to the enemy, and he would thus have been able to eliminate us once and for all, or at least put us out of action for a long while, because the people would have been confused by the regime's granting a few concessions and it would have been harder for them to understand our views.

The October operations made it possible to shatter the enemy maneuver and Sandinismo appeared on the scene with renewed vigor. Also, in military terms it was not a complete failure. We weren't able to capture the Masaya garrison but at least most of the attackers survived. In the north the guerrillas remained active from October to May 1978 on what was called the Carlos Fonseca Northern Front. A few comrades were killed in the attack on San Carlos, but it was a military victory for us. We weren't able to hold on to it, but it wasn't like the attack on the Moncada in Cuba, in 1953;* we were able to strike, pull back, accumulate forces, and strike once again.

To prove the point, four months later we captured two cities and encircled an antiguerrilla camp in the Nueva Segovia area for the first time.

Had October been a failure, we would not have been able to undertake new actions in just a few months. From October on we grew in political and military strength all the time.

Harnecker: What about the masses in October?

Ortega: In October there was no mass response as far as active participation was concerned.

Harnecker: Then they were actions by a vanguard only?

Ortega: Yes, by a vanguard, which not only contributed to sharpening the crisis, frustrated the schemes of reaction, and enabled the vanguard to gather renewed strength, but also began to strengthen a series of activities that the masses had been carrying out, in spite of the repression, and which consisted of struggles for social gains, trade union and political struggles. Therefore, these actions strengthened the mass movement, which later became openly insurrectional.

Harnecker: But didn't the offensive lead to the adoption of even more repressive measures by the dictatorship?

Ortega: Yes. In its desperation, the regime adopted a series of indiscriminately repressive measures. The revolutionary movement was brutally repressed by the Somoza regime. The repression that had been gradually increasing became even sharper in retaliation for the October operations.

Harnecker: In that case wouldn't your operations be considered a sign of adventurism, resulting only in even stronger repression against the people?

Ortega: Yes. Some sectors of the left that were engaged in setting up trade unions, etc., claimed that those actions had destroyed the organization and the resurgence of the mass movement, but this wasn't so. It is true that the repression would affect the open, legal organization of the masses, but it wouldn't affect their organization under really revolutionary conditions. To go along with such claims would mean falling prey to the big show the imperialists were mounting with all the talk about the bourgeois-democratic way out, in which the trade union

*On July 26, 1953, Fidel Castro led a group of fewer than 200 in an unsuccessful attack on the Moncada garrison in Santiago de Cuba. Almost all were killed or captured; Castro was sentenced to fifteen years in prison for his part in the attack.

movement was to participate. For us it was preferable that such a castrated trade union movement not be formed.

Summing up, the big jump ahead occurred in October 1977 and this sharpened the crisis. Then came the assassination of Pedro Joaquín Chamorro, which made the situation even worse, and with the masses in the cities, in the neighborhoods, everywhere, participating more and more in the uprising, the process became completely irreversible.

After that came the capture of the city of Rivas along with the city of Granada on February 2, 1978. Present in these actions were several comrades who were later killed in the struggle, such as Commander Camilo Ortega Saavedra, who led the attack on Granada; the commander, guerrilla priest, and Spanish internationalist Gaspar García Laviana; and Panchito Gutiérrez, among others.

Harnecker: When did the masses begin to join the insurrectional process?

Ortega: The operations of October 1977 gave a big boost to the mass movement, but it wasn't until after the asassination of Pedro Joaquín Chamorro that they really came out in full force and made crystal clear their potential, their determination, and their Sandinista will to join in the armed struggle.

I would like to make clear that the uprising of the masses as an aftermath to Chamorro's assassination was not led exclusively by the FSLN.

Harnecker: Was it a spontaneous action?

Ortega: It was a spontaneous reaction on the part of the masses which, in the end, the Sandinista Front began to direct through its activists and a number of military units. It was not a mass movement responding to a call by the Sandinistas; it was a response to a situation that nobody had foreseen.

Now then, our capacity for introducing ourselves into that mass movement was still limited at the time and was aimed at reaffirming our political and military presence among the masses, but not yet from a concrete organic standpoint because we didn't have the necessary cadres.

In October we began to take steps in that direction: the activists, the mechanisms — and new permanent forms of mass organization began to take shape quickly: the neighborhood committees, the work done in a number of factories and in the student movement. Furthermore, the United People's Movement was already beginning to take shape even before October. This was the result of the Sandinistas' efforts to regroup the revolutionary organizations around their program in order to fight against Somoza's regime and gradually lead the people in our process of national and social liberation.

When the bourgeois opposition sectors began to retreat during the strike, the FSLN made its presence felt with the armed actions of February 2. This is why we decided to capture Granada, Rivas, and the antiguerrilla camp in Santa Clara, Nueva Segovia.

The capture of the antiguerrilla camp was led by Germán Pomares, Victor Tirado, and Daniel Ortega. Camilo, our younger brother, led the attack on Granada, and the capture of Rivas was led by Edén Pastora and the priest Gaspar García Laviana.

It was the first really serious blow dealt in the crisis. These large-scale actions redoubled the masses' enthusiasm and their determination to fight Somoza. They now saw a strengthened vanguard capable of fighting, of dealing blows to the enemy, of capturing cities. In other words, the masses saw a considerable advance from the operations in October to these operations, in the same way they considered the operations in October to be a considerable advance over the previously defensive position of the Sandinistas. Therefore, we were gaining momentum, for the operations in February were superior to those in October.

Harnecker: Wouldn't the fact that you had to withdraw from the captured cities be considered a failure?

Ortega: No, not at all, because we took the cities, seized the weapons of the National Guard, overpowered them, harassed the enemy, and kept on hitting them every chance we got. Everybody stayed in or around the cities.

By then the Carlos Fonseca Column was operating in the northern part of the country, without having suffered a single tactical defeat.

At the same time, the guerrilla forces of the Pablo Ubeda Column, operating in the mountain areas, were able to get back together due to a respite in the intense pressure that the National Guard had been putting on them. The guerrilla movement in Nueva Segovia had much more effect on the vital economic, social, and political centers because it was operating nearer to them. But it was the traditional guerrilla movement and the movement in the mountains that made possible the growth and the moral and political hegemony of the Sandinista movement until October.

In other words, October was the continuation of the armed struggle mainly in the mountains because that was what the existing operational conditions called for, but the time came when the armed struggle had to be transferred to zones of greater political importance.

It wasn't a question of storing away what we had accumulated, but of reproducing it. If we remained there we'd be holding on to what we had but if we moved to other zones we'd be reproducing ourselves.

The greatest expression of the impact of the February actions is the insurrection of the Indians in Monimbó. It was the first of its kind, organized and planned ahead of time by the Indians and Sandinistas who were there. The battle lasted for almost a whole week, until February 26. The enemy crushed that uprising, which was partial —

Harnecker: You mean it was the only one in the whole country?

Ortega: Yes, but at the same time, that partial uprising was the soul of the masses on a nationwide scale and became the heart of the insurrection that was to take place throughout the country.

Harnecker: When you were planning the Monimbó uprising weren't you aware of the limitations of an isolated action?

Ortega: But we didn't plan the uprising. We just took the lead in the action that was decided upon by the Indian community.

The Monimbó uprising began around February 20 and continued for about a week. The capture of several cities (Rivas and Granada, for example) and the action carried out by the Northern Front had aroused a feeling of great expectation, of agitation among the masses, and the insurrectional propaganda spread by the FSLN beginning in October through pamphlets, etc. distributed throughout the country was beginning to bear fruit. The vanguard, however, hadn't been able to make contact in a more organic form with those sectors of the masses with the greatest political awareness. The actions of that sector, encouraged by the telling blows dealt the National Guard by the FSLN, in the midst of the Somoza regime's political crisis and the country's social and economic problems, surpassed the vanguard's capacity to channel all that popular agitation.

The neighborhood of Monimbó, which is a district of Masaya with some 20,000 inhabitants and both urban and rural zones, began in a spontaneous fashion to prepare for the insurrection. They began to organize block by block, set up barricades around the whole district, and take over the key spots. They also began to execute henchmen of the regime, to apply people's justice for the first time. They began to work as a Sandinista unit when they still lacked the organized leadership of the Sandinista movement.

And this doesn't mean that there were no Sandinistas there. There certainly were and that's precisely why Camilo Ortega went to Monimbó, with contacts we had there, to try to lead the uprising, and he was killed in the fighting.

Harnecker: I understand now. Therefore, it was not an uprising that you had planned. Now then, would you have stopped it if you had been able to do so?

Ortega: It would have been very difficult to do that, because the uprising responded to the objective development of the community. Of course, in keeping with our plans, maybe we would have postponed it or planned it differently. Maybe we wouldn't have organized an armed insurrection but rather some other kind of mass activity, but that's the way things turned out. This was the way this Indian sector responded immediately to the incentive provided by the capture of the cities by the FSLN several days before.

In late February the organization of the vanguard was still limited and we didn't have the cadres to channel the determination and fighting spirit that existed among the masses.

Harnecker: An isolated uprising like that one meant that the enemy could concentrate all its forces against it.

Ortega: Exactly, and that's something we learned by experience.

Harnecker: Then, it's important to know about other historical experiences in order to avoid making mistakes.

Ortega: Of course. We, the vanguard, knew of those historical experiences, but the masses didn't.

Harnecker: So it was actually a lesson for the people.

Ortega: Yes. We, the vanguard, knew it from the classics. The principle of concentration of forces has been one of the basic principles in warfare since ancient times.

What's important is that, in our case, we went through that experience in spite of the vanguard. The vanguard was certain that the uprising would be a setback, but a setback that would be transitory, because the decision of Monimbó contributed to raising the morale of the rest of the people who joined the uprising.

To what extent can the action be considered to have been a historical mistake? To what extent was the action an error on the part of the people, or was it simply their only option at that time? The fact remains that that example contributed both nationally and internationally to the development and ultimate triumph of the insurrection. Perhaps without that painful step which entailed great sacrifice it would have been more difficult to achieve that moral authority, that arousal among the country's masses, that spirit of support for one another that came from having witnessed how they had sacrificed themselves to win the support of the whole world for a people that were waging a struggle singlehanded. Perhaps without that example it would have been more difficult to speed up the conditions for the uprising.

That was an experience we and the people learned from.

With the experience we had acquired from October to Monimbó we were able to verify that the masses were willing to stage an uprising, but they needed more military organization, more mass organization. There was a need for riper political conditions and there was a need for more agitation, for better means of propaganda, such as a clandestine radio station.

It was necessary to mobilize the masses for war through the most elementary forms of organization.

Harnecker: You began to consider the matter of the radio station then?

Ortega: We'd been thinking about it since October but we hadn't been able to set it up. We had a radio set that the first anti-Somoza fighters had used in 1960, but it was old and we weren't able to put it in working order at that time.

However, we managed to fix it later and we put it in operation in those months of 1978. It was heard in Rivas, but very faintly. By then we were fully aware of the need for a radio station, of a way to communicate with the masses in order to prepare them for the insurrection.

But to get back to the idea I was developing. A gradual strengthening of forces was achieved amidst an enormous amount of activity that included the execution of Gen. Regualdo Pérez Vega, chief of the General Staff of the National Guard, the capture of the palace in August* and winding up the first stage of this insurrectional movement that had begun in October 1977, with the nationwide uprising in September 1978.

Harnecker: At that time, when you issued a call for the uprising, did you think it would be successful?

Ortega: We issued a call for the uprising. A series of events, of objective conditions, came up all of a sudden that prevented us from being better prepared. We could not stop the insurrection. The mass movement went beyond the vanguard's capacity to take the lead. We certainly could not oppose that mass movement, stop that avalanche. On the contrary, we had to put ourselves at the forefront in order to lead it and channel it to a certain extent.

In this sense, the vanguard, aware of its limitations, decided to adopt the general decision taken by the masses; a general decision that was based on the example of the Indians of Monimbó, who, in

---

*In August 1978, twenty-five FSLN guerrillas took over the National Palace, and held hostage more than sixty members of Somoza's puppet Chamber of Deputies. They succeeded in winning the release of sixty political prisoners, having three Sandinista communiqués read over the radio, and obtaining a large ransom.

turn, had been inspired by the example of the vanguard.

In other words, the vanguard set the example in October; the masses followed suit for the first time in an organized fashion in Monimbó. The vanguard created the conditions on the basis of that example and the masses moved faster than the vanguard because a whole series of objective conditions existed, such as the social crisis, the economic crisis, and the political crisis of the Somoza regime.

And since the regime was in such a state of decomposition, every one of our actions far surpassed the impact we expected would result from them. But we had to keep on hitting. It was very difficult to hit the target. We hit it, but it wasn't precisely a bulls-eye.

We were inspired by a spirit of victory, but we were aware of our limitations. We knew that it would be difficult to win, but we had to wage the struggle with that kind of spirit, because it's only with that spirit that people are prepared to shed their blood.

Furthermore, if we didn't organize that mass movement it would have fallen into general anarchy. In other words, the vanguard's decision to call for the uprising in September made it possible to harness the avalanche, to organize the uprising for the victory that was to follow.

Harnecker: What conditions were ripe for insurrection?

Ortega: The objective conditions of social and political crisis existed. But the conditions of the vanguard, in terms of the organizational level to lead the masses, and especially in terms of weapons, did not exist.

We didn't have the necessary weapons but everything else was ripe.

Harnecker: There was a very significant economic crisis, but Somoza still held many elements of power, chiefly the army —

Ortega: Right, exactly, the army. And we didn't have the experience of participating in a national uprising, the training such an experience gives the masses and the knowledge of the enemy, who showed up all his weaknesses. We didn't have enough weapons, but we did know that even if the uprising was not victorious it would be a blow from which the regime would never recover. We were absolutely convinced of this and so great was our conviction that a month later we were already calling for insurrection again.

There were some comrades on the left who held the view that September practically negated all possibility of a short-term victory, that the operations had been a strategic mistake, a defeat, and they thus had delayed the day of victory.

They were mistaken because September was not a victory but it wasn't a defeat in strategic terms either. It was a historical achievement with both positive and negative aspects.

Harnecker: So, what is the final verdict, then?

Ortega: That it was an accomplishment, because we grew as a vanguard. One hundred and fifty men participated in that uprising and our forces were multiplied several times over: three- or fourfold, plus the potential for recruiting thousands of others. We grew in size and in firepower because we captured weapons from the enemy. The vanguard suffered very few casualties. There were people killed as a result of Somoza's genocide, but very few cadres were killed in combat. In other words, we were able to preserve our strength.

Harnecker: What is your verdict from the military standpoint?

Ortega: We preserved our forces, acquired military experience, captured weapons, learned about the enemy, and destroyed some of the enemy's means of mobilization, including armored vehicles. The enemy suffered more casualties than we did; the people had a hand in this as did our own firepower, and we were able to retreat — this is a great lesson — successfully. For the first time we were able to engage in military maneuvers, pulling back to other places in the city and countryside to accumulate forces for the new insurrectional struggles of an offensive nature which soon materialized.

So, we can't say it was a defeat. It would have been a defeat if they had exterminated us, if they had seized all our weapons, if we had been broken up and dispersed.

It was not a military victory since we were unable to capture the garrisons in the five cities where there was fighting, but it was a significant political accomplishment.

I repeat, we called for insurrection because of the political situation which had developed and to prevent the people from being massacred alone, because the people, just like they did in Monimbó, were taking to the streets on their own.

Harnecker: Wouldn't the people have been massacred just the same, with or without you?

Ortega: No, it would have been worse, because at least we channeled the will of the people, just as happened in Monimbó, but on a much larger scale. That is why I told you we went forward; we never went around in circles.

In the final stages, the peasants came down to join the struggle in the cities. In Chinandega, the safe houses were filled with people taking three-hour classes. The people were going to take to the street: The people were the ones in the vanguard of that struggle. There was no alternative but to put oneself at the head of that upsurge and try to obtain the most positive outcome.

We placed ourselves at the head of that movement and led it in five cities. It was the first national uprising led by the FSLN but that was chiefly due to pressure by the masses.

Harnecker: You mean that on calling for insurrection you took into account above all the mood of the masses.

Ortega: That's right, because their morale was high and became higher when the palace was captured in August — that paved the way for the September insurrection.

Harnecker: When you planned the capture of the palace, did you consider the impact this would have on the masses?

Ortega: We knew the mass movement was coming to a head, but we preferred that it come to a head than that it not come to a head.

The important thing was to foil the imperialist plot which consisted of staging a coup in August to put a civilian-military regime in power and thus put a damper on the revolutionary struggle.

The palace operation had to do with the plot. We felt that since we didn't have a large-scale party organization, since the working class and the working people in general were not well organized, the only way to make ourselves felt in political terms was with weapons. That's why we carried out many operations that were military in form, but profoundly political in content. That was the case in August.

It was a military operation which was an outgrowth of a political rather than a military situation. That was also the case in October 1977 when we had to regain the military initiative and counteract a political maneuver.

Harnecker: So, when some people ask why you called for the September uprising without having achieved the unity of the three tendencies, this is explained by —

Ortega: Conditions for unity did not exist then. First we had to strengthen the struggle, and all the tendencies were working on this.

Little by little we came to an understanding but around a line which was called for in practice; it was not our line but the one the people demanded.

After Monimbó we dissolved the Carlos Fonseca Column and sent its members to the nerve centers of economic, social, and political activity in the country. As far as we were concerned there was no choosing between mountain and city; it was a case of being with the masses.

We sent some of the forty men in the column to Estelí, others to Managua, and others to León — The column served as a means to educate people. It made possible more all-around training because they were gathered there under the wing of members of the leadership like Germán Pomares and other members of our national leadership. That was how we trained a small group of cadres whom we later sent to the cities to prepare the insurrection, using what we learned in Monimbó.

Given all that had happened from October to Monimbó, we held the view that it was necessary to put ourselves at the head of the mass movement in order to prevent the repressive forces from wearing it down, because if that had happened, no matter how many guerrilla columns we had, victory in the short term was out of the question.

The crux of victory was not military in nature, it was the masses' participation in the insurrectional situation. We always struggled to keep the activity of the masses going, and at the end it was showing signs of decline, given the fact that there had been two years of uninterrupted activity after October and repression was getting steadily worse. National Guard members would dress up as guerrillas, and, since nighttime belonged to the guerrillas, they would move into neighborhoods and kill people.

The repression was so severe that some people were starting to fall back.

As far as we were concerned, the entire strategy, all the political and military steps taken were focused on the masses, on preventing a decline in their morale. This is why we undertook operations that did not fit within a specific political-military plan but they did serve the purpose of continuing to motivate the masses, to keep the mass movement going in the cities, which, in turn, allowed us to gain in strength. The masses made it possible for the armed movement to accumulate the forces the masses themselves needed.

We strived to keep the masses in action. That's why at times it seemed as though operations were disconnected from a military plan. But, in fact, they were in line with a political-military strategic situation aimed at keeping the mass movement going because that was the only way to obtain a military victory.

Our insurrectional strategy was centered on the masses not on military considerations. It's important to understand that.

Harnecker: But didn't the fact that the emphasis was on urban insurrection as opposed to the guerrilla column lead to an unduly great loss of life and destruction? The fact that the struggle was centered on the cities makes it easier to repress, for example the bombing of the cities —

Ortega: That question is meaningless, because that was the only way to win in Nicaragua. If it had been otherwise, there would never have been a victory. We simply paid the price of freedom. Had there been a less costly means, we would have used it but reality showed us that in order to win we had to base ourselves on situations that had been taking shape, for better or for worse, in a disorderly manner and which implied a very high social price.

Trying to tell the masses that the cost was very high and that they should seek another way would have meant the defeat of the revolutionary movement and more than that: falling into utopianism, paternalism, and idealism.

Liberation movements must realize that their struggle will be even more costly than ours. I personally can't imagine a victory in Latin America or anywhere else without the large-scale participation of the masses and without a total economic, political, and social crisis similar to the one in Nicaragua.

I myself feel it is very difficult to take power without a creative com-, bination of all forms of struggle wherever they can take place: countryside, city, town, neighborhood, mountain, etc., but always based on the idea that the mass movement is the focal point of the struggle and not the vanguard with the masses limited to merely supporting it.

Our experience showed that it is possible to combine the struggle in the city and in the countryside. We had struggle in the cities, struggle for the control of means of communication, and struggle in the guerrilla columns in the rural and mountainous areas. But the columns were not the determining factor in bringing about victory; they were simply part of a greater determining factor which was the armed struggle of the masses. That was the main contribution.

In May, after the September developments, the movement gained in military and political strength, the activity of the masses became more far-reaching, the barricades were erected, the daily struggle in the neighborhoods continued. None of this would have been possible had there been a strategic defeat.

From September until we launched the offensive in May, the brunt of military activity was borne by the guerrilla columns of the Northern Front and the ones in Nueva Guinea, in rural and mountainous areas. The final offensive began with the capture of El Jícaro, in Nueva Segovia. In March Commander Germán Pomares was active in the area and was able to overpower the enemy garrison and set several ambushes for National Guard contingents coming to aid the forces defeated at El Jícaro. These operations continued with the capture of Estelí in April by the Carlos Fonseca Northern Front column. Estelí was taken by a guerrilla column, not an uprising. The masses joined in afterwards.

Harnecker: But why did you capture a single city again? Isn't that a repetition of the Monimbó experience?

Ortega: No, because we weren't defeated in Estelí; the National Guard was unable to rout the guerrilla fighters there. Our comrades withdrew by breaking through the encirclement and demonstrated that thousands of soldiers had been unable to defeat a column of less than 200 men. It's true that the forces used in the capture of Estelí should have been larger. What happened was that orders had been given to carry out a series of operations in the area of Estelí and our comrades launched a direct attack on the city. These were actions that were within the perimeter of the Northern Front; they were mutual support operations between the forces of the Northern Front. But the situation in the country had deteriorated to such an extent that the capture of the city created a nationwide feeling of expectation that accelerated the insurrectional offensive.

After September the brunt of the war was borne by the guerrilla columns of the Northern Front. At the same time, all over the country the militia and the combat units of the Sandinista forces continued to harass the enemy. Hundreds of the regime's henchmen and informers were executed. After the insurrection the people realized that they had won and were incensed by the repression.

Harnecker: In other words, the blows that were being dealt the enemy had a greater effect than the repression?

Ortega: A much greater effect. By this time the people were already experienced in battle and their thirst for victory was so great that the September crimes, rather than dampening their spirit, strengthened it even more. Everybody had had a relative or friend killed in the struggle and there was a great thirst for revenge. The people wanted revenge and we weren't going to go against their wishes.

The final offensive began in March 1979 with the capture of El Jícaro. The different tendencies were beginning to unite by then. Everybody was in favor of beginning an offensive in the north, and there was a general consensus regarding the uprising. The capture of El Jícaro was followed by that of Estelí. After Estelí there was Nueva Guinea, a military setback for us, but it served to bog the enemy down, to wear him down. It cost us 128 men — The plan was correct, but our comrades were unable to cope with a number of tactical problems and the enemy hit them hard.

Harnecker: What was the plan for Nueva Guinea?

Ortega: To infiltrate a column there, to bog the enemy down, to carry out guerrilla operations. This would create the conditions in the rest of the country for carrying out political-military work in the cities once the National Guard was dispersed. The repression would be less because the National Guard would be bogged down in Nueva Guinea. But instead of sticking to guerrilla warfare, our comrades operated on flat terrain and became an easy target for the enemy.

Harnecker: In other words, by then the center of the struggle had shifted to the guerrilla units.

Ortega: The mass movement did not allow the enemy to concentrate all its military force against the columns and, at the same time, the columns' operations forced the enemy to go out in search of them. This, in turn, made the mass struggle in the cities a little easier.

The enemy found himself in a dead end. If he left the cities, the mass movement would get the upper hand, and if he remained, this would help the guerrilla columns' operations.

Harnecker: This way of organizing the armed struggle, was it planned beforehand or was it something that you learned as you went along?

Ortega: Well, these are things that you learn in the course of the struggle and use to your advantage. We knew that it would be that way. We planned an operation in the north to force the National Guard to go there, giving us a chance to better organize the rest of the country.

Harnecker: However, that statement you made about the mass struggle in the cities making it possible for the guerrillas to gain military strength is a conclusion you arrived at later. You didn't plan it that way, did you?

Ortega: You're right. It was a conclusion based on practical experience. Getting back to the series of operations, after Nueva Guinea we captured Jinotega in May and this was followed by the battle in El Naranjo, on the Southern Front. It was then that we called for the final uprising.

Harnecker: What made you issue the call for the insurrection in May?

Ortega: Because by then a whole series of objective conditions were coming to a head: the economic crisis, the devaluation of the córdoba, the political crisis. And also because, after September, we realized that it was necessary to strategically combine, in both time and space, the uprising of the masses throughout the country, the offensive by the Front's military forces, and the nationwide strike in which the employers, as well, were involved or in agreement.

There would be no victory unless we succeeded in combining these three strategic factors in the same time and space. There had already been several nationwide strikes, but not combined with the masses' offensive. There had been mass uprisings, but not combined with the strike or with the vanguard's capacity to hit the enemy hard. And the vanguard had already dealt blows, but the other two factors had been absent.

These three factors were combined to a certain extent in September, but not completely, because the process still wasn't being led entirely by us. We made it clear after September, in an internal circular, that there would be no victory unless these three factors were combined.

It would have been very difficult, without the Sandinistas' unity, to gather and synthesize into a single practical line all the achievements that the various tendencies had accumulated. This is why we can say with certainty that unity played and will continue to play a major role in the revolution.

Harnecker: But shouldn't there have been still another factor? I'm saying this because — at least from the outside — there seemed to be a balance of forces that was very difficult to break.

Ortega: Well, that's the military aspect. I'll explain that later. Now we're dealing with the strategic factors. From a strategic standpoint, as of May, Somoza had already lost the war. It was only a question of time.

Harnecker: But if you hadn't received the weapons you received in those last few weeks would you have been able to win?

Ortega: I'll go into that presently, but first I want to say that it's very important to combine these three factors. After September we captured El Jícaro and we tried to take Estelí, too, but we couldn't coordinate the operation well. Later, Estelí was captured, and this was practically an action by the vanguard, a hard blow, but still another isolated action. The Nueva Guinea operation was aimed at supporting Estelí but the forces in Estelí were already withdrawing. The operation in Nueva Guinea aroused nationwide interest, and when the forces were being mobilized to continue the advance, to combine all those factors, Nueva Guinea fell and then came Jinotega, which arose in an attempt to coordinate it with Nueva Guinea and then gradually coordinate everything.

The taking of Jinotega coincided with the activity on the Southern Front and the capture of El Naranjo — on the Costa Rican border, where the National Guard had stationed a large force — which the Southern Front's general staff decided to capture in coordination with an attack on the city of Rivas, thus beginning the final offensive on the Southern Front of Nicaragua.

The Southern Front wanted to take advantage of the dispersion of the enemy forces resulting from the capture of Jinotega, but when it went into action the forces in Jinotega had already withdrawn. That was the action in which Germán Pomares was killed.

We came to the conclusion that if we continued this way the enemy would cut us to pieces, because they would be weakening us bit by bit.

If we lost El Naranjo we would lose the chance of scoring a short-term military victory. We just couldn't afford to lose at El Naranjo. We worked out a plan that, at that time, concerned chiefly the internal front, that is, the fronts having to do mainly with the cities, since at that time the guerrilla columns were dispersed and recovering from the battles they had fought and, therefore, wouldn't be able to go into action immediately. Thus, the insurrection was launched with the full awareness that the columns of the Northern Front, in the mountainous areas, would not be able to take part in the action immediately but would do so later.

The way we saw it, the insurrection had to last, at a nationwide level, for at least two weeks in order to give the columns a chance to regroup and go into action at the right moment, making the enemy's situation completely untenable and subjecting the enemy to a constant strategic siege, with victory only a question of time, of wearing down the enemy before launching the final attack. We planned to wear down the enemy by cutting off his means of communication, isolating his military units, cutting off supplies and so forth, thus forming a nationwide battlefront that the Somoza regime wouldn't be able to cope with.

And that's just what happened. We worked out the insurrectional plan. What was planned, basically for the cities, was that when the Benjamín Zeledón Column of the Southern Front went into action in El Naranjo, the uprising was to be launched a few days later in the Rigoberto López Pérez Western Front, which would create a very difficult situation for the National Guard: major blows in the North, blows in the West, and more blows in the South. Several days after the battles in El Naranjo, our forces in Masaya, Granada, and Carazo were to go into action, cutting off the means of communication to Somoza's forces on the Southern Front. The uprising in Managua was to start as soon as fighting had begun on all those fronts.

Harnecker: Excuse me for interrupting, but wasn't it in El Naranjo that the Sandinista forces were defeated and had to retreat?

Ortega: No. We didn't suffer a defeat at El Naranjo. What happened there was a military maneuver; that is, we left the El Naranjo hills, and several days later we captured Peñas Blancas and Sapoa, the National Guard's major military bases on the Southern Front. We succeeded in getting Commander Bravo out of Sapoa and after that we waged a positional war in the entire area until the war was over.

Harnecker: Going back to my question about the military balance of forces and the matter of weapons, what was your original plan?

Ortega: We planned to seize our weapons from the enemy.

Harnecker: But it didn't turn out that way.

Ortega: Well, it did, in part. This is what actually happened: beginning with the actions in El Naranjo, we succeeded in launching the offensive by the vanguard and coordinating with the other fronts. We succeeded in calling a strike, which turned out to be a general strike and in which Radio Sandino played a decisive role. Without the radio station it would have been difficult to keep the strike going. The mass insurrection also took place. Therefore, the three factors we were talking about were combined. After that, when Somoza began to get bogged down and was unable to destroy our forces, his defeat was only a matter of time, in fact, a matter of days. The strategic situation was already defined. From a strategic standpoint, the enemy had lost; they were only defending themselves, but we couldn't win either, due to a question of firepower. Solving this problem made it possible to hasten the end of a war that the enemy had already lost. They could still win a few battles, but never the war. Somoza would never have been able to get out of the hole he was in. Now then, if we hadn't had that armament, maybe the war would have lasted longer, had a higher social cost, caused more bloodshed and greater destruction. With less armament we would have won anyway, but at the cost of greater destruction.

We got the weapons but they didn't reach all the places they were needed; and in those places it was possible to defeat the National Guard by resorting to destruction, by burning entire city blocks in order to surround the army garrison by fire. Wherever there was an army garrison and we didn't have enough weapons, we got the people out of their houses — which were already practically destroyed by the enemy's bombs and mortar shells — and we proceeded to occupy the houses nearest the garrison in order to bring our forces up close and keep it under control. The houses that were already destroyed were set afire to force the enemy to abandon the surrounded garrison.

What few weapons we had we deployed near the exit and other key spots, and we fought the enemy with contact bombs. In other words, thousands of people fought with machetes, picks and shovels, and homemade bombs. That was the armament and it showed that it was capable of destroying and was destroying the enemy, except that it meant a longer war. Only a solution to the problem of firepower could hasten the end of a war that the enemy had already lost.

By then Somoza had no foodstuffs, no gasoline, couldn't use any of the highways, could no longer control the country; the economy was already in ruins, everything was paralyzed. Somoza could no longer rule and his position was untenable. To this we should add the international pressure. It was only a question of time before Somoza was overthrown.

Harnecker: But couldn't that time factor also be harmful to the mass movement by drawing all the strength out of it?

Ortega: No. At that stage of the game there was no danger of its being exhausted, because even though there weren't enough weapons, they were being captured from the enemy and the enemy was being defeated. Needless to say, the armament that was received played quite a decisive role in hastening the victory and, in some cases, in deciding a few battles which otherwise would have been lost. We don't know if losing those battles would have had any effect on the spirit of the masses and on the military situation in the rest of the country and we would have lost the war. In this sense, we can say that the armament played a strategic role and that it is necessary to have a minimum reserve of war matériel — bazookas, explosives, and armament with high firepower — rather than large quantities because they would never be enough to meet the needs of the people. What counts is the people's will to go out into the streets and fight with whatever they have at hand.

To sum up, it was possible to combine those three factors — strike, insurrection, and military offensive — and, before that, the unity of Sandinismo was achieved, without which it would have been difficult to keep those factors combined and coordinated. Furthermore, there was an excellent rearguard network that made it possible to have the technical backing necessary to end the war quickly. The means of communication were also of vital importance: wireless for coordination among the various fronts, and the radio. Without them it would have been impossible to win the war, because it would have been impossible to coordinate it either from a political or military standpoint. We succeeded in organizing Radio Sandino, which was the main means of propaganda for the uprising and for the strike. Another factor was our ability to maintain broad alliances, a policy that succeeded in isolating the Somoza regime, achieving nationwide anti-Somoza unity, and neutralizing the reactionary currents in favor of intervention.

Without the monolithic unity of the Sandinistas; without an insurrectional strategy supported by the masses; without the necessary coordination between the guerrilla fronts and the military fronts in the cities; without effective wireless communication to coordinate all the fronts; without a radio broadcasting system to guide the mass movement; without hard-hitting technical and military resources; without a solid rear guard for introducing these resources and preparing the men, training them; without prior training; without previous victories and setbacks as happened in Nicaragua beginning in October 1977, when the masses were subjected to the most savage repression which was, at the same time, a great source of learning; without a flexible, intelligent, and mature policy of alliances on both the national and international levels there would have been no revolutionary victory. The victory was the culmination of all those factors.

It all sounds very simple, but you can't imagine what it cost us to do it — It cost us an October, a February, a palace, an insurrection in September, all the battles after September in El Jícaro, Estelí, Nueva Guinea. It cost us all the efforts made in the zone of the Pablo Ubeda Column in the mountains, in the Atlantic Coast zone. That's what we had to pay for our victory.

Harnecker: About the rear guard — something that was absent in many Latin American guerrilla movements — when did you start organizing it?

Ortega: We always had a rear guard. The movement had direct experience with a rear guard dating back many years. Our country is not an island like Cuba, we have to rely on neighboring countries, and the revolutionary movement relied on support from the neighboring movements from the very beginning. Sandino himself went to Mexico, to Honduras — many Hondurans and Costa Ricans joined Sandino's struggle — so we counted on support from Honduras and Costa Rica to meet some needs of the rear guard that were difficult to meet in Nicaragua.

We operated clandestinely in Costa Rica and Honduras. And in order to set up the rear guard at higher levels it became necessary — along with finding resources and setting up clandestine schools — to begin arousing — to begin arousing a feeling of solidarity with our cause among the main progressive political sectors in each country, without being sectarian, and not with the left-wing sectors alone, because that would have meant isolating ourselves. Nobody gave us a rear guard; we won the right to have one.

The alliances we achieved through our efforts were of vital importance in our obtaining heavy weapons and sophisticated equipment.

Harnecker: Considering that yours was an armed movement, how did you manage to put into practice a broad policy of alliances? It would seem easier for an election-oriented movement to put into practice a policy of that kind.

Ortega: We succeeded because we earned respect for ourselves, and this is something that other movements have not achieved; they are not taken seriously, they are not respected. We won the right to establish alliances, we imposed our right. If they hadn't seen us as a force to be reckoned with they wouldn't have approached us, but they realized we constituted a force and thus had to become our allies. And they did so due to our political program, even though ours was an armed movement with a revolutionary leadership.

The progressives realized that ours was a revolutionary movement and that we weren't totally in accord with their ideology, but they also realized that we had a political program that was, to a certain extent, of interest to them and that we had military power. Those three factors made it possible for us to establish true alliances, not paper ones. We made no agreement of any kind. We just set down the rules of the game and acted accordingly, and as a result we went on gaining political ground.

Harnecker: Can you tell us what effect the international balance of forces had on your victory?

Ortega: The international balance of forces, the international situation, the state of the various forces in the area, the contradictions of Western developed countries, etc., must definitely be taken into account.

It would have been very difficult for us to win by depending only on internal development. We realized that the internal gains had to be reinforced by the forces that existed abroad. And the only way to achieve this was to practice a mature, flexible policy by disclosing our revolutionary, democratic, and patriotic program for national reconstruction. That was what made it possible for us to count on the support of all the mature forces the world over, the revolutionary forces, the progressive forces.

Harnecker: Mature forces, you say? What do you mean by this?

Ortega: I'm speaking of the bourgeois forces that go through a process of maturity and don't rush into adventurous undertakings like those of the CIA and the reactionary sectors. There are mature forces in the world that, realizing the quality and strength of a revolutionary movement, even if they have contradictory interests, end up respecting it. It is even possible, in fact, to form certain alliances, to agree on certain political issues, that have a bearing on the balance of forces necessary for the final attack. In order to achieve this it is important to have a program which responds to the country's real problems, that proposes solutions that everybody will consider correct.

We defined the objective problems: that Nicaragua must undergo reconstruction for such and such reasons, that national unity was necessary for such and such a reason and so forth —

Moreover, it was necessary to win everybody's support, not the support of the left-wing sectors alone. The Sandinista Front made it a point to set up an infrastructure of solidarity in each country, seeking, firstly, the support of all; and secondly, the support of those who best understood our problems.

Now then, there's a big difference between sympathizing with our cause and providing material aid. And who's going to provide such material support? Whoever wants to do so, without political commitments of any kind attached, without jeopardizing principles.

Getting that support was a great accomplishment on the part of the Sandinistas. We wanted to get as much support as we could abroad in order to frustrate any scheme of foreign intervention. And in doing so we even won the support of sectors in the United States itself.

Harnecker: As far as the Sandinista movement is concerned, what bearing did the existence of the three tendencies and their later reunification have on the process?

Ortega: As I said, Sandinista unity was a decisive factor in the victory. However, in order to understand the process of reintegration we must go back a bit into history.

What happened in Nicaragua was not a profound division in the FSLN but rather a sort of split-up of the vanguard into three parts as a result of our lack of maturity at the time —

Harnecker: When did that happen?

Ortega: It started between 1976 and 1977.

Harnecker: And what was the reason for it?

Ortega: I was coming to that. More than a question of ideology, of program, it was a question of the leaders' concern over finding a solution to the problems of the revolutionary movement and channeling the revolutionary activities in that direction.

Harnecker: I don't quite understand what you mean —

Ortega: Well, the leadership's way of dealing with the problems was primitive. In actual practice, there was virtually no coordinated leadership. As a result of the repression and due to the fact that we remained out of contact with one another for long periods of time, plus the lack of a common line, of a political commitment set down in writing, everyone worked as they pleased. And this led to clashes. The split was not caused by profound ideological and political differences, although this type of problem did exist. If we had been better organized, perhaps we could have settled the contradictions — which are always present in the initial stages of every movement — in a positive manner, encouraging criticism while maintaining unity. The lack of this necessary framework for discussion along with our immaturity as individuals, as revolutionaries, coupled with the repressive atmosphere led to our gradual split, breaking up into the three tendencies that everybody knows about.

The split coincided with the death in combat of Oscar Turcios and Ricardo Morales, both members of the national leadership. It arose out of the growth of the Sandinista movement itself, and came at a time when the very development of the movement called for a radical improvement in our organization and leadership, a more organized vanguard capable of effectively leading the mass struggle, of charting a sure path for the armed struggle in Nicaragua. We were aware of this need, but we were not able to accomplish this, to assimilate the experience of our older comrades — more experienced in party work, in working with the masses, with more military experience and more experience in dealing with political forces at home and abroad — and to combine this with the dynamism of the young people who were already beginning to join the movement in significant numbers.

It was necessary to combine the old with the new and, in practice, this created clashes. The older comrades began to mistrust the younger ones, who were beginning to assume responsibility for a number of tasks, and the young ones, who had no idea how hard the struggles of the preceding years had been, underrated the older comrades because the veterans still resorted to primitive methods of work which the young ones thought should be eliminated.

Harnecker: You consider yourself among the veterans?

Ortega: Wouldn't you say so? I was among those who started years ago.

Harnecker: How do you explain the implicit division of labor between the three tendencies by virtue of which the Proletarian Tendency worked chiefly with the urban masses and the Prolonged People's War Tendency with the guerrillas in the mountains?

Ortega: I want to explain that the division of labor of which you speak was not the result of the division into tendencies; it existed before the division of the front.

Let me explain —

The leaders of the three tendencies were concerned with the overall problems of the revolution. What I'm trying to say is that when, at the time of the split, the comrades working on the different tasks assigned to them by the FSLN realized that they were unable to come up with solutions for the problems they faced — because of the drawbacks and weaknesses I've already mentioned — they started to organize themselves and the work they had mastered on the spot and seek solutions to the problems they faced according to the structures within their reach. You must remember that we were working amidst brutal repression; it was impossible to do nationwide work, everybody worked according to what the situation dictated. The comrades who worked in the mountains continued doing so in line with the prevailing situation; those who worked more closely with sectors in production, with students, and in making known scientific revolutionary theory continued to do so; and those who had been doing chiefly military work, seeking insurrection, pursued that line.

Actually the efforts made by the three separate structures were furthering a single struggle, were giving rise to a single policy, and were evolving a single strategy for victory.

That explains why none of the tendencies thought of setting up a new FSLN.

Harnecker: So you didn't have three general secretaries —

Ortega: Of course not. And that explains why, when the unity of the movement was reestablished, the work the three tendencies had done was complementary.

Harnecker: So this sort of division of labor existed before the split —

Ortega: Yes, the different areas of work had been decided upon by the movement. The fact that we all came from a common root was very helpful. It led us to respect the work of the other tendencies. For example, the insurrectional tendency did not try to set up another revolutionary student front. It let that organization, which played such an important role in Nicaragua, remain under the control of the other tendencies. Nor was there any interference with the work the "Proletarian" comrades did in several factories, and they didn't interfere either. They didn't try to set up another Northern or Southern Front, which was the most important military work done by the "insurrectionals." The efforts were coordinated and they complemented each other.

Harnecker: Besides, no one of the three could have triumphed without the help of the others.

Ortega: That's right. The problem was that each one wanted to lead the process, wanted to be the one that stood out the most, but that was overcome in the course of the struggle itself and everybody realized the importance of everybody else's work. Thus we came to the unity agreements which we started to work on in late 1978 and which were concluded in March 1979, based on a single policy, without anyone having to give ground to the other. The whole Sandinista movement agreed on a single policy which upheld the insurrectional nature of the struggle, called for a flexible policy on alliances and the need for a broad-based program, etc. This programmatic, political, and ideological foundation made it possible for us to coordinate our efforts with increasing effectiveness and pave the way for our regrouping. I think it would be more correct to say that we regrouped together rather than reunited. The three tendencies all had a great desire to become a single FSLN once again, as shown by the enthusiasm, love, and zeal with which this unity is preserved now, and we're sure it is irreversible. Just as Sandinista unity was vital for victory, the unity of all the left around Sandinismo and of the entire population around the left and Sandinismo is vital to consolidate the process and achieve our goals.

Harnecker: We understand that women played a very important role in the armed struggle in Nicaragua, that in the cities they fought shoulder to shoulder with men and in the columns they came to constitute 25 percent of the force; that there were several women commanders. What are your views on this? Was it something new or was there a tradition of women participating in such activities?

Ortega: The Sandinista Front was heir to the tradition of women's participation in the struggle, not only in Sandino's time but also in the past century and even further back. You already know about the role of women during Sandino's struggle, of his comrade, of internationalist comrades like the Lía Toro sisters. Or the case of the women who were murdered by the Yankees in 1912. There was a woman from El Salvador involved; her name was Lucía Matamoros. She was drawn and quartered for having fought against the intervention of that time. There was also Comrade Concepción Alday, the wife of the first Liberal guerrilla to fight the Yankees in Chinandega, who was killed in 1926.

The FSLN inherited and followed up on this participation. But it's important to point out that Sandinismo not only developed the participation of women in the vanguard organization but in all sectors, and not just in support work for key tasks but in key strategic tasks. Such is the case of guerrilla Commander Dora Téllez, better known as Commander 2; guerrilla Commander Mónica Baltodano; and other guerrilla commanders such as Leticia Herrera. These three comrades played a very important role, not just in support work for the revolutionary struggle but as political and military leaders. In the course of the insurrection, they were leaders on the battlefield, as in the case of Dora Téllez (Claudia), who headed what was called the Rigoberto López Pérez Western Front, one of the most important fronts of the war.

Sandinismo did not close the doors to women's participation; that would have been a backward, sexist way of underestimating them. Women played a very important role in the insurrection. There were columns in which all the officers were women, women who commanded hundreds of men without any problem.

Harnecker: Before we end this interview, would you like to say anything else?

Ortega: Well, first of all, I would like to thank you for this opportunity to discuss these issues, which are vital to an understanding of our revolutionary process. I would have liked to give more thought to the answers but the daily tasks we face have made this impossible. What I said here should not be viewed as the last word, as the definitive analysis. I've just expressed my particular views, which I hope will contribute to a better understanding of our process, of our brave and inspiring revolutionary struggle.

On Human Rights in Nicaragua

by Tomás Borge

The following presentation was made by FSLN leader Tomás Borge, Nicaraguan minister of the interior, to the Inter-American Human Rights Commission on October 10, 1980. The commission spent a week in Nicaragua, meeting with representatives of the government, the armed forces, the judicial system, and the Catholic church, as well as with ex-National Guard prisoners and their families. On its departure, the commission announced it would recommend international humanitarian aid to Nicaragua.

This presentation was originally published as a pamphlet by the Ministry of the Interior. The translation is by Intercontinental Press.

We have listened with great respect and attention to your opinions. Perhaps I should start by saying that in every country there are only two possibilities. Either you are in favor of human dignity and respect for human rights, or you are against human rights. There is no other possibility.

Leaving aside the nuances that may exist, and without being mechanical about it — either you're for human rights or you're against them.

The political thrust of this revolution and this government is unshakably and irreversibly in favor of human dignity, of human rights. Obviously, in practice we have fallen short of perfection, but the most important thing is our strategic, historic decision to be in favor of human rights.

Our inviting you here was one result of this decision.

In order to talk about human rights, you have to talk about the Somoza dictatorship, and about all the governments Nicaragua has had. But especially about the Somoza dictatorship.

Over the last half century our people have been put in front of the firing squad without any legal niceties being observed. They have been put into torture chambers.

The Somoza government's specialty was violating all the laws — even those laws that existed in the country at the time, which are not the same as the laws that exist today. Now we see the contradictions between the laws of the past and the revolution that is under way. We haven't yet had time to change the entire judicial system, but we know that much of it is obsolete and not in line with our revolutionary principles. There was a legal framework under the dictatorship, but Somoza just did not pay much attention to it.

The abuses committed under Somoza are familiar to all of you — even though a criminal like Somoza does everything possible to hide his crimes. When he was in power, he was able to cover up a lot of things.

As a matter of principle we have not tried to hide anything, not even our mistakes, not even the abuses that have been committed. But in the days of the dictatorship, obviously, everything possible was done to cover up the worst aspects of the repression.

You never had a chance to talk to the peasants who had grease spread on their genitals so that the dogs would eat them. You could not talk to the men who were scalped alive with razors and had salt and vinegar rubbed into their wounds so they would suffer until they died. You certainly never had a chance to talk to the peasant women who were raped, as almost 100 percent of them were in some northern provinces.

Probably you don't even know about the peasants who were buried alive in the mountains. You don't know the incredibly horrible statistics on the number of victims. You have spoken of the large number of victims — we know that they numbered in the tens of thousands. More than 100,000 Nicaraguans were killed.

Think about the fact that there wasn't a single family in Nicaragua that escaped the repression, not even the family of Somoza himself. Because Edgar Lang, a Sandinista martyr and hero, was a relative of Somoza's; many members of Somoza's family were victims of repression.

Repression under Somoza went so far beyond the normal limits that it touched his own family and the families of friends. There wasn't even a single Somozaist family that escaped the repression. That gives you some idea of the magnitude of repression under Somoza.

Of course all this repression led to an enormous buildup of resentment and hatred in the Nicaraguan population. Everything that has to do with the National Guard is despised in this country. We made a big effort to save some members of the National Guard. We found them jobs, and in some cases the workers accepted them out of a sense of discipline. But they wouldn't talk to the Guardsmen — they turned their backs on them and made their lives miserable.

People will not put up with the *guardias* for the reasons I have already explained. Because besides being murderers, they were thieves. Besides being robbers, they were brutal. They killed a lot of Nicaraguans, and they stole the property of others.

They were murderers, thieves, torturers, and rapists. That's what they were. That's what they still are in the places they have fled to.

Perhaps the worst crime Somoza and his son committed was not that of killing Nicaraguans, not that of turning the National Guard into criminals, but that of turning *children* into criminals.

You refer to the youngsters who are in prison — the specialty of those children was gouging out prisoners' eyes with a spoon. This was one of the techniques of these children who were horribly deformed by Somozaism.

But the revolution has made a political decision not to put these youngsters on trial but to try to rehabilitate them.

Unfortunately some of them were taken to the facilities where the adults are. The revolution is setting up separate facilities for them, but in the meantime they have a separate section of the Modelo facility; they are not with the others. We want to get them out of there, and we will do so as soon as we have another place for them.

Right now we cannot afford the luxury of just turning them loose, because they would become delinquents. These youngsters — without work and with all the deformations they have suffered — would become murderers and thieves and would end up back in jail for new crimes. For this reason we wouldn't be doing them any favor. We are going to take them someplace and rehabilitate them.

Our revolution has historically had a policy of not executing anyone. Those were the instructions we gave during the war. It is not just something we decided after our victory, but a policy we followed during the war itself.

I don't know if the tape recording still exists of a speech I made to the National Guard when we had them surrounded in the barracks at Matagalpa. It went out over the radio, over our own radio. In it I told them to turn themselves in, that nothing would happen to them. The National Guard never believed us when we told them this.

I remember when I was taken prisoner. I was brutally tortured, kept with a hood over my head for nine months, and kept handcuffed for seven months.

I remember when we captured those who had tortured me. I told them: "I am going to get back at you; now comes the hour of my re-

venge, and my revenge is that we are not going to harm a single hair
on your heads. You didn't believe us before, but now we are going to
make you believe us."

That was our philosophy; that was the way we were. But take a min-
ute to think about what it meant, what it means to have been in Nicaragua in those days.

You, Mr. President* — just imagine that they murdered your wife,
the way they murdered mine. Imagine if they had brutally murdered
your son or your brother, if they had raped your wife or sister or
daughter — and then you came to power.

This will give you some idea of the moral stature of the leaders of
this revolution, that we have not taken revenge against those who did
us so much harm.

But we cannot demand the same consciousness from the great mass
of fighters who saw their brothers and sons shot down, whose wives
were raped, whose daughters were raped, whose loved ones were tortured, who were themselves victims of torture, who lived through the
frightening destruction of the bombs that fell in their cities and of the
rockets that fell on their houses and killed children and old people.

They came to power with the sound of shots still ringing in their
ears, still feeling the blood recently spilled and the crimes just committed.

The logical, natural thing to do was to turn the guns against those
who had lived by the gun. But the immense majority of the National
Guard were not shot; only a tiny minority of these murderers were
shot. Even we ourselves don't know who they were. It was like *Fuenteovejuna* — everyone was in it together.**

When the revolution won, they gave me a million córdobas to start
setting up the Ministry of the Interior. And I started spending this money to set up a police force and State Security, without bothering to
ask for receipts. I don't know exactly what happened to this money. If I
had to give an exact accounting, they would have to send me to jail.

You cannot have the faintest idea of the situation that existed in Nicaragua at that moment. I don't even know who was in charge of the
La Pólvora barracks right then — and I don't think anyone knows.

*Commission President Thomas Farer, a U.S. citizen.

**Fuenteovejuna* is the title of a 1618 drama by the Spanish writer Lope de Ve-
ga about the murder of an oppressive tax collector in the village of Fuenteovejuna. When questioned by the king's prosecutor, the villagers take collective responsibility for the act.

People spent one week here and the next week someplace else.

All right, it is possible that if we were to make an investigation we might be able to find out who was in charge of La Pólvora.

But do we really have the moral right to punish those who fought alongside the people against the tyranny, who risked their lives, who perhaps were wounded, who saw their fathers and brothers and sons killed?

What right do we have to ask now that they be punished for things that happened at a time when there were no mechanisms of control in the whole country — when there existed neither judicial order nor military order.

These compañeros did not have a very clear idea of what they were supposed to be doing, and some may even have thought they were following the policy of the revolutionary government. The means of communication we had at our disposal to let people know what the policy was were not very good, and this was also true during the war.

It would be very difficult for us to track down who was responsible for the things that happened in the first months after the victory, extremely difficult.

We would be demagogues and liars if we told you we were going to punish these compañeros, if we told you that we were going to have a thorough investigation to find out who was responsible for the executions that took place in the days after the victory.

On the other hand, we have punished a lot of people. When we found out about something, we penalized those responsible. But we did not publicize what we were doing, and I don't even remember the names of those penalized.

We deported one fighter, whose name I don't remember, a South American, who I found committing abuses. We immediately expelled him from the country.

We also put in jail some compañeros whom we found committing abuses. I don't know if they are out now.

But you don't have any idea of what those first months after the revolution were like: there wasn't the slightest bit of control over anything.

When we founded the Ministry of the Interior, there were six of us; and in the whole country there was no police force, no State Security, no judges, no courts, no Supreme Court, no nothing.

All we had were titles: "You're the minister of the interior." "You're the president of the Supreme Court." There was no infrastructure. We didn't even have offices. We didn't have files. We had nothing, absolutely nothing.

About the only thing we could do then was go around here and there trying to stop bad things from being done.

When they tried to lynch the prisoners who were in the Red Cross building, I personally went to see the relatives of our martyrs who were there ready to take their revenge.

I needed all the powers of persuasion I possessed. I didn't tape record what I said, but I think it was one of the most eloquent of the few eloquent speeches I have made in my life.

In any case, I managed to persuade them not to kill the National Guard. Mr. Ismael Reyes, who is a member of the Red Cross, was there; he was the one who called me.

There was a large crowd trying to break down the doors to get in and kill the murderers who were inside. We were able to convince them not to do it. We were able to convince them by saying that we could not kill them because we had made this revolution in order to put a stop to killings.

This was perhaps the most persuasive argument. I asked them: "So why did we make this revolution, if we are going to do the same thing they used to do? If that's the way it is going to be, we would be better off not having made the revolution."

We said the same thing to the police, to members of the State Security, to the compañeros in the army: "Don't commit abuses; don't be disrespectful to anyone; don't hit prisoners." Because often they did hit prisoners or kill prisoners. *We said to them: "If you do such things, then what did we make this revolution for?"*

It was a battle, a tremendous battle. We asked the Church to help us. For example, we asked the Church to help us improve prison conditions. One time a German clergyman came to this very office and expressed his admiration for the revolution and asked me: "How can we help you?"

We told him: We're going to tell you a secret; we want you to help us to improve conditions for the prisoners.

We didn't want to say it publicly, because several times when we did something to improve conditions, word got out. And people didn't like it.

If you were Nicaraguan and you had suffered all that Nicaraguans have suffered, you wouldn't be very sympathetic with the idea of doing something for the prisoners either. When we ask people what we should do with the prisoners, they say, "Shoot them." If we had gone along with the will of the people on this, we would have shot them all.

That is why we told this clergyman to help us improve the conditions of the prisoners. We told him: "Don't send us aid for our children, whom we love more than anything in the world. Send us aid for the prisoners, for the criminals we are holding in jail, for the murderers."

Some Christian businessmen came, some North American millionaires, including an astronaut who had been to the moon, and they asked us what they could do to help. We told them also: "Build us the best prison in Latin America, the most humane, because we want to set an example for the world in our treatment of prisoners."

They promised; we'll see if they keep their word. I hope they do, because they gave me the impression of being serious and responsible people. So far they have sent us 7,000 Bibles, which we have divided up among the prisoners.

We have some serious problems with our prisons. There aren't very many of them, and they are in poor condition. There is overcrowding; there are shortages of foodstuffs. The staff suffers from these problems as well as the prisoners.

One time I almost started to cry — not for the prisoners, to tell the truth, but for the compañeros who were guarding the prisoners. It seemed like the compañeros were the prisoners and the prisoners were the ones standing guard. The prisoners were better off than the guards, who were sleeping on the floor, half-naked, with no shoes, half-dead with hunger. It was a pitiful picture.

This is a country that was left in ruins. It is important not to forget this fact. This is a country reduced to rubble. We have extraordinary problems, yet efforts are being made to improve the prisoners' conditions.

We are battling not only to improve their material conditions but also to counter the hatred that the compañeros watching them feel toward them.

We are the ones carrying out this battle, because we have the moral authority to do it. But if I had been a National Guardsman or a Somozaist, or one who was indifferent, I wouldn't have much moral authority to ask the compañeros to treat prisoners well.

But we ourselves were the victims of the National Guard, we were tortured, we and our families were victims. For that reason we do have the moral authority to ask that they be treated well.

No one can accuse us of having a selfish interest in having them treated well, because if we had any selfish interest it would be in having them treated badly.

We can expect some improvements. The problem of overcrowding can be reduced by building more prisons. That's the only way.

We built one new prison. We invested a million and a half córdobas, and when it was finished it turned out the engineer — who was obviously incompetent — hadn't designed in sewers. And other experts we consulted came to the conclusion that it was impossible to put in sewers because of the condition of the ground.

So months of work came to nothing, along with our expectations of moving the prisoners into better quarters where we had planned for them to have conjugal visits and other basic rights we want to introduce into our penal system.

Now we have to begin looking for other possible locations for a place we can put them for at least a few months. The engineer inspector says that we can't take anyone over to the Granada facility. In the meantime, we have given instructions that the prisoners be permitted more frequent visits.

Yesterday I was in Jinotepe prison, and I found out that we need better communications. We still haven't perfected our means of communication. They hadn't yet gotten the order we issued some time ago to allow more frequent visits, or the order to permit the prisoners to receive magazines and books and other things. We also found some prisoners who were being held unjustly and released them.

We agree completely with the idea of increasing the number of visits the prisoners are allowed. But you should be aware that there are administrative problems related to such visits.

The Tipitapa prison, for example, has a capacity of 700. That is, it should have 700 but it actually has more than 2,000.

It is difficult to control visits under such conditions. It can only be done by increasing the staff. This means spending more money, but we are going to find ways to allow more visits.

We have already authorized more frequent visits, as well as the right to walk freely through the halls, and to receive books, newspapers, magazines, cigarettes, radios, television, and other things that were prohibited before, such as bringing in lemons and oranges and other fruits. All this has now been authorized.

It is true that the compañeros in charge of the penal system have established some rules that are somewhat mechanical and sometimes even childish. One time I visited the prison in Granada, where I learned of a rule that every time an official came by, the prisoners had to stand at attention.

One official named Leana went by 300 times a day. So every time she went by the women were supposed to stand at attention. It was ridiculous.

We still haven't straightened out things like that, much less perfected all the administrative and institutional norms of the country. But we are making a lot of progress.

We are going to release more prisoners. We have already released a lot. What happens is that we make the mistake of not letting people know about the disciplinary measures taken against many compañeros for abusing prisoners, and we also have not made public the number of prisoners we have released. We have freed thousands of prisoners.

We only made it public in the first few days, when I freed more than a hundred criminals, ex-Guardsmen, from Jinotega. Today, by the way, they are listed among the "disappeared"; actually, they fled to Honduras. We also have not publicized a lot of the disciplinary steps taken. Commander Cuadra has given you just a few examples of people disciplined under the law.

We are going to free all those prisoners whose physical condition prevents them from posing any danger, regardless of what they have done, unless the charges against them are very serious indeed.

I have been thinking that even though we had decided not to free a lot of the women prisoners until the Human Rights Commission left, that, given the productive discussions we have had, and the positive attitudes you have shown, we should free them immediately. And I am going to propose this to the government.

We are going to make a study. We will send lawyers to all the prisons to look into the possibility of freeing a lot more prisoners.

It wasn't possible in the very beginning to tell who was telling the truth and who wasn't. Many of the prisoners even changed their names. Their relatives come to the prisons and look for them under their real names, and they "can't find them."

These prisoners are deathly afraid of the revolution. They are afraid because of the crimes they committed. They have guilt complexes, and that's why they won't give their real names.

You will also find if you study the answers they gave to the Special Tribunals, that they were all cooks, typists, bartenders, barbers, and mechanics. Nobody ever fired a shot. You would think that we had just been shooting at ourselves.

Some would say, "they only recruited me three days before." Others claimed to have been in the army only a month; others said they had deserted; others that they were really in the FSLN. Ferreting out the truth in all these cases is very difficult.

We are, however, training groups of compañeros. We have given them instruction in judicial norms, in respect for human rights, in questioning prisoners, so that we can speed up the trials. Now more are being held than before.

In the beginning it was a big problem, but now we are getting more experienced in such procedures. Every day we do them a little better, and now we are preparing thirty-five new people.

As I told you, it's a hard job. We started out with no experience. Who were the judges in this country? Who had any judicial experience in Nicaragua? The Somozaists, and their experience was all in the framework of corruption.

The only thing we knew how to do was fight. We are still half guerrillas. We weren't judges, we had no legal experience. We weren't investigators, we weren't police, we weren't anything. We have learned all this under the gun.

It is a little more than a year since the victory, and from a historical point of view this is only an instant, only a historical second. We ourselves have said that we are only beginning to normalize things, to create a state apparatus.

We have special interests of our own. For example, we are interested in building the FSLN. But the FSLN is waiting on the sidelines while we take care of our immediate task of organizing the state apparatus. We can't do anything without a state structure.

July 19 came this year and we were just getting around to paying attention to the FSLN as a political organization. Why? Because we didn't have a state. We are just now beginning to have a real state.

And the first priorities of the state were not in the judicial system — they were in health care, the literacy crusade, and defense of the revolution.

Now that we've achieved some normalcy in defense and in health and education, we can start. We can start to give the legal system its proper importance. Up to this point it hasn't had a single vehicle, or its own building; now we're providing vehicles and giving them a building. We're starting to give some encouragement to those in charge of the judicial system; we are meeting with them more frequently. Before we couldn't, because we had other things to do.

With the end of Somoza's dictatorship came the end of the legal structure and coercive forces that supported Somoza. We were faced not only with the job of reconstructing buildings destroyed by the war but also of building a state apparatus, and the latter is sometimes as difficult as the former.

There are some people who feel nervous about what is happening, but perhaps the first thing we have to say is that there has been a revolution here. And a revolution makes some people very happy and others not so happy. There are some who feel very secure about it and others very insecure.

There is a new sense of security among the immense majority of the population, who used to live in fear. They were always afraid of being killed, of being thrown in jail, of being tortured, afraid their lands would be stolen, afraid they would lose their jobs or be kicked out of school. They lived in a state of extreme insecurity.

But who was responsible for this insecurity? The social groups that ruled the country. Now those who were insecure before have recovered a sense of security; they feel safe for the first time.

But those who before caused insecurity to the big majority of the population now feel insecure themselves — even though this revolution has been extremely flexible and has given everyone an opportunity. They feel insecure even though we have seriously proposed — and this is not just a tactical or short-term thing — that we maintain a mixed economy and political pluralism.

We mean it when we talk about political pluralism and a mixed economy. But what happens is that a thief thinks everyone else is like him. And these people think we are tricking them, when in fact we are going to great pains to show them that we are not lying, that in fact they are the ones who historically have been the liars. They can't concede the possibility that there might be people who aren't liars, and therefore they feel nervous.

Obviously this is a vicious circle, because this insecurity they feel causes them to decapitalize their businesses. But when they begin to do that, their workers become aware of what they are doing. And then the revolutionary government becomes concerned.

We are not prepared to allow them to decapitalize their businesses. Such a lack of confidence is a blow to this country. They are all in debt, which is the best proof. There is not a single private enterprise in this country which is not in debt to the financial system.

And it would not even be a radical step, but a simple business procedure, for us to say to them: "Gentlemen, either you pay us or you turn over your operations." But they aren't in a position to pay.

So what has the revolutionary government done? Has it taken away their businesses? No. In fact it has extended them more loans in order for them to develop their businesses.

Unfortunately, we have a backward capitalist class. I want to be frank with you. I think that in the long run a certain segment of the so-called private sector is going to come to its senses. There are some people who don't show good sense now but may some day come to their senses. There are some who are half-sensible who may become sensible; just like there are some who already show some common sense in which this characteristic may become stronger.

We could have wiped these people out. We had the power to do it.

This would only have shown that we had as little sense as they do. But we have learned something from history. People learn from experience. We have learned that in order to be revolutionaries and advance a revolutionary process, it is necessary to have one's feet on the ground.

We could have taken away all their businesses and we would not have been overthrown; I'm sure of that. But what is most conducive to the economic development of the country is what is best for the Nicaraguan people. So when we talk about a mixed economy, we mean it; and when we talk about political pluralism, we mean it.

This is not a short-term maneuver but our strategic approach. The political approach of the FSLN is to maintain a mixed economy and political pluralism.

We are not going to violate these principles. But we are not going to let them decapitalize their businesses, because that means taking resources out of the country and destroying those enterprises.

We want to see the development of private enterprise, private commerce, and private cultivation of the land. Furthermore, we have no interest in nationalizing the land. On the contrary, we are interested in expanding private ownership of the land. We think this should be basically in the form of cooperatives, but if there are also private enterprises involved in agricultural production, we want them to develop too.

We will give them whatever help they need, just like we did to the San Antonio sugar mill, for example, which is a million-dollar operation in private hands.

We are going to multiply the number of cooperatives, which is a form of private ownership of the land, and one that people only join on a voluntary basis.

Cooperatives are nothing unusual; they aren't communism, like some backward elements here think who don't have the faintest idea what a cooperative is. You only have to read half a page of a book on the subject to be aware that a cooperative involves private ownership.

There is a political uncertainty among certain sectors. The traditional parties in this country — and I'm not talking about the traditional parties just to attack them — have ruled Nicaragua for more than a hundred years and they have never been able to solve the country's problems. But they want to go on living. They stubbornly refuse to retire to a museum.

We are not going to prevent them from continuing to live. They are going to die a natural death, and new, modern, different parties need to come into being.

The Liberals* don't dare to identify themselves, but there are those who are bold enough to suggest that the Liberals should be a political option in this country. This doesn't worry us.

What kind of influence can these parties have, either historically or among the masses? They are doing us a big favor by presenting themselves as our opposition. We'd rather have them for an opposition than some modern party with relevant ideas and a possibility of a future.

Better them than new sectors that aren't tainted with having been Somoza's yes-men, having made deals with Somoza, having been part of the reactionary hysteria that prevailed in this country. Tainted by complicity with the imperialist interventions in Nicaragua (with all due respect to our honored friend, the president of the commission). This is the kind of opposition we don't have to worry about. They are the ones who are worried.

At a certain time, they were demanding immediate elections. We said no, and one of the reasons was precisely because we favor political pluralism.

If we had held elections six months after the victory, or if we held them right now, those people wouldn't even get half a deputy. Political pluralism would disappear. If there were 100 representatives in congress, it would be 100 Sandinistas. And since we do favor political pluralism, we want them to have political representation; we would like them to be able to organize themselves into some type of party that would at least have the possibility of presenting itself as an option.

Besides that, we really didn't have time to spend holding elections right then. It would have meant an expenditure of energy and resources when our main job right then was to get our economy going again.

But elections will be held. We have already set the date. That will be the time to have a contest in the electoral arena. What won't be up for debate is whether or not there is a revolution in Nicaragua.

We have publicly criticized people in the private sector, but they have criticized us as well. They demand the right to attack us, but they don't think we have a right to attack them.

If they can attack us, why can't we do the same to them? If they call us communists, why can't we call them reactionaries? If they say we've sold ourselves for gold from Moscow, why can't we say they are prostitutes who have sold themselves to imperialism?

If they have the same right to express themselves as we do, and they attack us in *La Prensa* and over Radio Corporación and other stations, then we can attack them in our media.

*Somoza's party.

We can defend ourselves and we can criticize them. But we do it with the truth, and they do it with lies.

But all right, everyone has their own idea of what truth is. Some people think lies are the truth.

It is true that certain means of communication, such as Radio Sandino, belong to the FSLN, just like Radio Corporación belongs to the reactionaries. It is also true that other means of mass communication, such as television, are in the hands of the state.

I wish you would ask the French why they control certain communications media. Television, for example, is in the hands of the state in France — and not only in France but in Spain too, just like in Nicaragua. The reason is that the television stations belonged to Somoza, and what was Somoza's passed into the hands of the new state. If there had been a television channel in private hands, it would still be in private hands.

But at this point we are not in favor of licensing a new commercial television station, because we are trying to transform Nicaraguan television. Traditionally, television has been very alienating. Alienating because it encourages pornography, because it glorifies crime and violence. We are making a big effort to transform television into something educational, because television is a very effective medium of communication.

What we can consider is opening up television to other political forces, such as the Church. We have nothing against the idea of the Church having access to television. The Human Rights Commission headed by Dr. Leonte Herdocia has already suggested it.

There has been some discussion about the scope of our laws on state security. The problem is that we don't have all the state structures we need in this country, and the laws that do exist aren't always useful. There is a contradiction between the new revolutionary structures that have arisen and the judicial system. For example, in the old days, criminals were arrested and then freed because they bribed the judges. The lawyers and legal experts all went along with this. The police went along with it. Because of all this, prisoners were set free.

In December we are going to issue some pardons. We are going to assign some people to make as careful a study as possible of each prisoner's case. We want to free those who are physically incapacitated and those who clearly are not guilty. We also want to study the cases of a lot of those who were tried in the first months, because some of them might have been given excessive sentences. It may be that in some cases we will reduce the sentences.

We don't have a new system of laws written since the revolution. This is a very big problem. We still have judges who aren't very honest. This is because in order to have honest judges you have to have honest lawyers. One day we went out with a lamp looking for an honest lawyer in Nicaragua. We found just one — we found Leonte Herdocia.

Maybe I am exaggerating. Maybe there are a number of honest lawyers, but the number is not very big. They were trained in a horribly corrupt school. The problem with Nicaragua is that corruption was so pervasive that being corrupt was not considered strange. In fact, it was being *honest* that was considered weird. Anybody who didn't steal was considered a fool.

I remember people talking about a man who worked in a bank and didn't steal, and they called him a blithering idiot. In other words, it was sort of a crime not to be a criminal. People acquired very negative habits. We need new generations to overcome this, to forge new attitudes.

A lot of lawyers bribe judges. They try to get money from the family of someone who is arrested. The police don't have very good investigative techniques, they don't produce evidence in time, so, as a result, someone walks off scot-free who is obviously a very dangerous individual. So someone who has raped a three-year-old girl goes free for lack of adequate evidence, especially since there is a tendency to consider crimes like this a private business.

Edén Pastora caught a man with a gun in his hand attacking someone. He took away his gun and arrested him, but the man was set free for lack of proof. There are people who sell narcotics, a crime for which we have a special hatred, and they go free for lack of evidence.

Sometimes there are protests because the people don't want to let such people go, because they know for a fact the criminals will go out in the streets and commit new crimes. So sometimes they try to take matters into their own hands. We find the same type of resistance on the part of the chiefs of police in the provinces.

We have had certain problems with the judicial structure, trying to come up with laws that are strict enough so that criminals will be locked up and not left to hurt people. But writing laws is a difficult undertaking. Changing the judicial structure of a country takes time.

In the case of the Special Tribunals, you shouldn't think we aren't concerned about speeding things up. And the way we go about writing new laws (which are already better than they used to be) is more careful every day, in terms of the types of legal solutions to the various orders and cases that come up. Remember that the Special Tribunals deal only with crimes committed before the revolution.

Regardless of what they say about us, we are operating within a certain legal framework. It is possible to behave in an intelligent manner and still be true to one's principles. It is also possible to be true to one's principles and behave stupidly. Our inclination is always to tell the truth. We have demonstrated that it is much better to tell the truth, because you get in less trouble telling the truth than you do lying. It is almost always smarter to tell the truth.

There is a tendency, however, to try to cover up mistakes, and to exaggerate. I remember when we were in prison and the Red Cross came to interview us. Even though we were honest — some compañeros did exaggerate, a few did make up experiences.

I want to tell you something that will show how far we are prepared to go in being honest: I mentioned to some of you that the prisoners at Tipitapa now have it worse than we did when we were prisoners there. We were better off than they are. We were allowed weekly visits — I'm talking about Tipitapa.

Crazy things would happen. I remember one day they wouldn't let me have a book on psychic energy because they thought I would use it to escape. Another time they brought me a copy of *Capital* and said, "This one we'll let through because it's about capitalism."

We've already said that we are letting them have any kind of books except for comics and pornography. But we still were better off. Not me perhaps, since I was kept isolated, in a cell by myself, but the vast majority of us were better off than the prisoners are now. The main reason is that now there are so many people in jail. There weren't so many before and obviously it is easier to provide for a small number than a big crowd. When we were imprisoned at the place you visited, El Chipote, we were kept with hoods over our heads, in handcuffs, and they beat us every day. We all wanted to be sent to Tipitapa, because for us being at Tipitapa was almost like being free. There was such an enormous difference that being transferred to Tipitapa was almost like being let out on the street.

Now the opposite is true. Those who are in El Chipote don't want to go to Tipitapa; and those at Tipitapa want to go back to El Chipote. That is the difference.

They would rather go back to the State Security facility, which is more comfortable because there aren't so many prisoners. At El Chipote they can make their own meals and get what they want, but not at Tipitapa. There conditions are much worse.

I am telling you this because I imagine a number of prisoners and their relatives have told you about abuses they have suffered. They exaggerate of course, although in some cases abuses have been committed, which have been inflated by the prisoners.

Someone was asking about the abuses we have committed. I have to say there isn't a pattern of abuse. One day I went to a jail and a woman prisoner told me she had been undressed and forced to do situps in her underwear. I asked her to tell me who did it. The person she accused denied it, but she insisted.

I must say that the person accused was not a Nicaraguan; I think he was a Colombian. He was one of the remnants of the "Simón Bolívar Brigade."* We immediately deported him; this happened in the first few months.

It was very difficult to arrest people and put them in jail. We already had plenty of prisoners to worry about without going around arresting our own people. Besides, if we had put everyone who committed abuses in prison, I think we would have had to jail half a million Nicaraguans.

People not only committed abuses. They also stole cars, and looted abandoned houses. There wasn't a house that wasn't looted. Who did it? The people did it, our compañeros, the police, members of the army. Incredible things went on in this country.

It seemed like the most natural thing in the world to grab everything you could in these houses and make off with it. It was like communal property.

We lost a lot economically through the looting and destruction of buildings. This very building was stripped down to the walls. Everything was taken — air conditioners, toilets.

The house of the millionaire Montealegre, out on the highway to the

---

*The Simón Bolívar Brigade was an armed international contingent that entered Nicaragua in the closing days of the civil war; ostensibly to support the FSLN. While it utilized the FSLN's name and banners, the Brigade refused to submit to the discipline of the FSLN and carried out work in conflict with the FSLN's efforts. A provocation involving a demonstration organized by the Brigade and the Brigade's refusal to submit its armed units to the central command of the FSLN led to the expulsion from the country of its non-Nicaraguan members in August 1979.

The Simón Bolívar Brigade was organized from Colombia by followers of Nahuel Moreno, leader of the Bolshevik Faction of the Fourth International. Moreno's maneuver was launched without consultation with the elected leadership bodies of the International, which condemned the Brigade as a "criminal adventure." The Bolshevik Faction split from the Fourth International in November 1979.

south, was torn apart. We sent people to try to save the house, a house where there was a million-dollars worth of housewares alone. It was the house of a guy who spent three million córdobas on his daughter's wedding. It was a treasure.

Such houses should be taken care of. They belong to the people. This house became state property and we sent some people to guard it.

I went there a month later to see what there was, and everything was gone. They told me: "Someone came from the Ministry of Culture and said you had given them permission to take things out."

I don't know if they really were from the Ministry of Culture. The most natural thing in the world was to gather up things and take them away. This is called looting; it is called theft; and it is against the law in every country in the world.

Totally by accident, I found a broken painting thrown on the ground. It was a Picasso. I have since verified that it was a genuine Picasso. They didn't take the Picasso. This makes me think they weren't really from the Ministry of Culture, they were stupid.

This happened. The truth is that there was no control over anything. We set up a body called Cocoabe, but some of its members committed abuses. In those first days people would steal a car, and when it ran out of gas abandon it and steal another.

They wrecked a lot of Mercedes-Benzes, luxury cars. They totaled them, ran them into things. They would get out of a car after crashing it into something, and stop another car coming down the street, make the driver get out, and drive off in it. They would see a car parked and take it. Besides that, they would drive at incredible speeds. People were killed, there were accidents.

There is a psychological explanation for all this. People felt for the first time as if they were the bosses in their own country. It was a country that had always before been someone else's — it wasn't our country, it was almost like a foreign country. We were like foreigners here; it was like we were visitors in Nicaragua. And besides, we were discriminated against by the real rulers of the country, who weren't even Nicaraguan. Then, all at once, our people felt like the country belonged to them — the streets, the highways. They began to kill themselves driving around like lunatics. They began to take the things they had always been denied. These were people who had never had anything, and they suddenly felt like they ruled the world. They did a lot of damage to the country's economy, but this situation could not have been avoided.

There was only one thing we could prevent — the killing of the National Guard. Some were killed, but nothing like the number that would have been killed.

If we had given the slightest sign, not one Guardsmen would have been left alive. If we had gone along with it in the slightest way, every single one would be dead. But we were inflexible and took great pains not only to prevent them from being killed but even to see that they weren't mistreated. And we succeeded as much as possible.

This was a major historical accomplishment. We did it because that's the way we were taught. Carlos Fonseca taught us. The revolution teaches respect for other people. And we also did it thinking about Latin America.

If we had made a revolution here that was bloody and vengeful, with firing squads and beatings, we would hurt the chances of revolutionary movements in other places. We would make it harder for them to find allies, we would frighten people in other countries.

Whenever there is revolutionary activity in Latin America, people will say — not simply that we wish the revolutionaries well — but that we are sending troops, that we are sending arms.

We have promised in all seriousness not to send arms or troops to help the Salvadorans, and we have kept our promise. Mr. Carter can rest assured that we are keeping our promise not to send arms to the Salvadorans.

There is not the slightest danger that someday it will be revealed that we sent arms, because we haven't sent arms. It would be irresponsible, completely irresponsible. Even if we don't have a tremendous amount of affection for Carter, we don't think the Salvadorans need them.

Just like we couldn't prevent looting, and couldn't throw the people responsible in jail, in the same way we couldn't prevent a certain number of prisoners from being killed or mistreated. Who did it? We don't know. The people did it; the people themselves did the looting; the people themselves did the killing. People who had suffered terribly over a long period of time. There was a virtual explosion in Nicaragua, and the only reason it wasn't worse was because of the good sense, maturity, and respect for humanity that motivate the leaders of the revolution.

For the same reason that we decided to respect human rights, we also decided to offer you the greatest possible freedom of movement. Even though we had some reservations, even though we were not too sure that the commission would act with the necessary objectivity and understanding.

You probably also came into the situation with some prejudices against us. But we see that your attitude is positive, that you are not trying to put us on trial but rather to encourage us in our respect for human rights.

Just respecting human rights isn't enough for us. We want to become a shining example for the whole continent in the area of human rights, and we are going to do it. When people talk about human rights, when people talk about respect for human rights, we want them to say — "like in Nicaragua." You can help us with this.

The Role of Religion in the New Nicaragua

The following statement by the National Directorate of the FSLN was published in the October 7, 1980, issue of Barricada. *The translation is by* Intercontinental Press.

For some time the enemies of our people — driven from power once and for all — have been carrying on an obstinate campaign of distortions and lies about various aspects of the revolution, with the aim of confusing the people. This campaign of ideological confusion seeks to promote anti-Sandinista fears and attitudes among the people, while at the same time politically wearing down the FSLN through interminable polemics that never seek honest conclusions, but in fact seek precisely the opposite.

The question of religion has a special place in these campaigns of confusion since a large percentage of the Nicaraguan people have very deep-rooted religious sentiments. In this regard, the reactionaries' efforts have been aimed at spreading the idea that the FSLN is using religion now in order to later suppress it. Clearly, the purpose of such propaganda is to manipulate our people's honest faith in order to provoke a *political* reaction against the FSLN and the revolution.

This campaign is particularly vicious because it takes up matters that touch very deep feelings of many Nicaraguans. Given the importance of the question, and in order to orient our membership, clarify things for our people, and prevent further manipulation of this subject, the National Directorate of the FSLN has decided to issue this document expressing its official position on religion.

Christian patriots and revolutionaries are an integral part of the Sandinista people's revolution, and they have been for many years. The participation of Christians — both lay people and clergy — in the FSLN and the Government of National Reconstruction is a logical outgrowth of their outstanding participation at the people's side throughout the struggle against the dictatorship.

Through their interpretation of their faith, many FSLN members and fighters were motivated to join the revolutionary struggle and therefore the FSLN. Many gave not only their valiant support to our cause, but were also examples of dedication, even to the point of shedding their blood to water the seed of liberation.

How could we forget our beloved martyrs Oscar Pérez Cassar, Oscar Robelo, Sergio Guerrero, Arlen Siu, Guadalupe Moreno, and Leonardo Matute, or the dozens of Messengers of the Word* murdered by the Somozaist National Guard in the mountains of our country, or so many other brothers and sisters.

We should give special mention to the revolutionary work and heroic sacrifice of Catholic priest and Sandinista member Gaspar García Laviana. He represented the highest synthesis of Christian vocation and revolutionary consciousness.

All these were humble men and women who knew how to fulfill their duty as patriots and revolutionaries without getting bogged down in long philosophical discussions. They now live eternally in the memory of the people, who will never forget their sacrifice.

But the participation of Christians was not limited to serving as fighters in the Sandinista Front. Many Christians, lay people and clergy, who never participated in the ranks of the FSLN although some were linked to it, professed and practiced their faith in accord with our people's need for liberation. The Catholic church and some evangelical churches even participated as institutions in the people's victory over the Somoza regime of terror.

On various occasions the Catholic bishops bravely denounced the crimes and abuses of the dictatorship. Monsignor Obando y Bravo and Monsignor Salazar y Espinoza, among others, were abused by Somozaist gangs. It was a group of priests and monks that exposed to the world the disappearance of 3,000 peasants in the mountains in the north of our country.

Many Christians of different denominations carried a liberating message to the people. Some even gave refuge and food to the Sandinistas who were mercilessly persecuted by Somozaism.

People gathered in the religious houses to hear underground news bulletins when the Somozaist repression prevented independent radio stations from broadcasting.

Because of their brave participation in the struggle, the Catholic church and Christians in general suffered persecution and death. Many religious figures also were mistreated, were expelled from our country, faced a thousand obstacles to the exercise of their Christian faith. Many religious buildings were broken into, pillaged, bombed,

*The "messengers of the word" were lay Christians who proselytized among peasants in the early 1970s. They often played a role in organizing opposition to the Somoza dictatorship in the countryside.

and assaulted in attempts to murder compañeros inside, as was the case with El Calvario Church in León and the chapels in the mountains.

To a degree unprecedented in any other revolutionary movement in Latin America and perhaps the world, Christians have been an integral part of our revolutionary history. This fact opens up new and interesting possibilities for the participation of Christians in revolutions in other places, not only during the struggle for power, but also later in the stage of building the new society.

In the new conditions that are posed by the revolutionary process, we Christian and non-Christian revolutionaries must come together around the task of providing continuity to this extremely valuable experience, extending it into the future. We must perfect the forms of conscious participation among all the revolutionaries in Nicaragua, whatever their philosophical positions and religious beliefs.

FSLN's positions on religion

1. The FSLN sees freedom to profess a religious faith as an inalienable right which is fully guaranteed by the revolutionary government. This principle was included in our revolutionary program long ago, and we will maintain it in practice in the future.* Furthermore, in the new Nicaragua no one can be discriminated against for publicly professing or spreading their religious beliefs. Those who profess no religious faith have the very same right.

2. Some authors have asserted that religion is a mechanism for spreading false consciousness among people, which serves to justify the exploitation of one class by another. This assertion undoubtedly has historic validity to the extent that in different historical epochs religion has served as a theoretical basis for political domination. Suffice it to recall the role that the missionaries played in the process of domination and colonization of the Indians of our country.

However, we Sandinistas state that our experience shows that when Christians, basing themselves on their faith, are capable of responding to the needs of the people and of history, those very beliefs lead them to revolutionary activism. Our experience shows us that one can be a believer and a consistent revolutionary at the same time, and that there is no insoluble contradiction between the two.

3. The FSLN is the organization of Nicaraguan revolutionaries, who have voluntarily come together to transform the social, economic,

*See p. 20.

and political situation in our country in line with a known program and strategy.

All those who agree with our objectives and proposals, and have the personal qualities demanded by our organization, have every right to participate actively in our ranks, whatever their religious beliefs. Evidence of this is provided by the fact that there are three Catholic priests in the Sandinista Assembly.

Many Christians are members of the FSLN, and there will be Christians within the Sandinista Front as long as there are revolutionary Christians in Nicaragua.

4. As a vanguard that is conscious of the immense responsibilities that have fallen upon its shoulders, the FSLN zealously seeks to maintain the strength and unity of its organization around the explicit objectives for which it was formed. Within the framework of the FSLN, there is no place for religious proselytism. This would undermine the specific character of our vanguard and introduce factors of disunity, since the Sandinista Front includes compañeros of various religions and none.

Outside the framework of the FSLN, Christian activists — whether they be priests, pastors, members of religious orders, or lay people — all have the right to express their convictions publicly. This cannot be used to detract from their work in the FSLN or from the confidence that they have gained as a result of their revolutionary activity.

5. The FSLN has a profound respect for all the religious celebrations and traditions of our people. It is striving to restore the true meaning of these occasions by attacking various evils and forms of corruption that were introduced into them in the past.

We feel that this respect must be expressed not only by insuring conditions for the free expression of these traditions, but also by seeing that they are not used for political or commercial ends. If in the future any Sandinista activist departs from this principle, we state now that this in no way represents the FSLN's position.

Of course, if other political parties or individuals try to turn the people's religious festivals or activities into political acts against the revolution (as has happened in some instances in the past), the FSLN declares it also has a right to defend the people and the revolution in these same conditions.

6. No Sandinista member should, in any official capacity, offer an opinion on the interpretation of religious questions that are solely the concern of the various churches. These questions must be decided by the Christians among themselves. If a Sandinista who is also a Christian intervenes in the polemics of that kind, he does so in a personal

capacity, in his capacity as a Christian.

7. Some reactionary ideologists have accused the FSLN of trying to divide the Church. Nothing could be further from the truth or more ill-intentioned than this accusation. If there are divisions within the religions, they exist completely independently of the will and activity of the FSLN.

A study of history shows that around big political events members of the Catholic church have always taken different and even contradictory positions. Missionaries came with the Spanish colonizers, and they used the cross to consecrate the slave labor that had been initiated by the sword. But against them arose the firmness of Bartolomé de las Casas, the defender of the Indians.*

In the beginning of the last century many priests fought for the independence of Central America, some with weapons in hand. And on the other extreme there were priests who defended the privileges of the crown in Latin America with equal vehemence.

After liberation from the colonial yoke, we find the anti-interventionist positions of Monsignor Pereira y Castellón, who called for defense of the nation's interests against the North American invasion. During the Somoza epoch the figure of Monsignor Calderón y Padilla stands out, attacking the Somozas' vice, corruption, and abuse of power against the poor.

And today there is the massive revolutionary commitment among revolutionary Christians.

Earlier we mentioned the participation of many Christians in the people's revolutionary struggle. But we must also point out that some, like León Pallais and others, remained at Somoza's side to the end.

We should not forget that in that period there were priests who proudly paraded their military ranks and official positions — of course no one demanded that they give up their posts. But we should also not forget that in contrast to these sad examples we have the immense figure of Gaspar García L. and so many other Sandinista martyrs of Christian origin.

This situation continues in the present stage. An immense majority of the Christians actively support and participate in the revolution. But there is also a minority that maintain political positions opposed to the revolution.

Naturally we Sandinistas are good friends of the revolutionary

*Bartolomé de las Casas (1474-1566), a Spanish Dominican, was known as the "protector of the Indians" for his defense of the rights of the Indians against the Spanish settlers.

Christians but not of the counterrevolutionaries, even though they call themselves Christians.

The FSLN, however, maintains communications on all levels with different Churches, with the ranks and the hierarchy, without regard to their political positions.

We do not foster or provoke activities to divide the Churches. That question is the exclusive concern of the Christians and does not involve political organizations. If divisions do exist, the Churches must look for the causes within themselves and not attribute them to supposed malicious outside influences. Speaking frankly, we would look kindly upon a Church that took part, in an unprejudiced, mature, and responsible manner, in the common effort to continually expand the dialogue and participation that our revolutionary process has opened.

8. Another matter that has recently been the subject of discussion is the participation of priests and members of religious orders in the Government of National Reconstruction. In regard to this, we declare that every Nicaraguan citizen has a right to participate in carrying out political affairs in our country, whatever their civil state, and the Government of National Reconstruction guarantees this right, which is backed up by the law.

The priest compañeros who have taken posts in the government, in response to the FSLN's call and their obligations as citizens, have thus far carried out extraordinary work. Facing great and difficult problems, our country needs the participation of all patriots to move forward. It especially needs those who had the chance to receive higher education, which was denied to the majority of our people.

Therefore, the FSLN will continue to ask all those lay and clerical citizens whose experience or qualifications might be needed for our process to participate.

If any of the religious compañeros decide to give up their governmental responsibilities for their own special reasons, that too is their right. Exercising the right to participate in and fulfill one's patriotic obligation is a matter of personal conscience.

9. The revolution and the state have origins, goals, and spheres of action that are different than those of religion. For the revolutionary state, religion is a personal matter. It is the concern of individuals, churches, and special associations organized around religous aims.

Like every modern state, the revolutionary state is secular and cannot adopt any religion because it is the representative of all the people, believers as well as nonbelievers.

By issuing this official communiqué, the National Directorate of the Sandinista National Liberation Front hopes not only to clarify the question under discussion, but also and especially to remind the revolutionary militants of the FSLN and the Churches of their duties and responsibilities in the construction of our country, which has been held down by 159 years of pillage, repression, and dependence.

Building Nicaragua's future is a historic challenge that transcends our borders and inspires other peoples in their struggle for liberation and to create the new man, and it is a right and a duty of all Nicaraguans, regardless of their religious beliefs.

Sandino Yesterday, Sandino Today, Sandino Always!

Free Homeland or Death!

Members of the FSLN's National Directorate at a February 1980 rally.

Nicaragua's Economy and the Fight Against Imperialism

by Jaime Wheelock

FSLN leader Jaime Wheelock is Nicaragua's minister of agricultural development. This speech was given to the First International Conference in Solidarity with Nicaragua, held in Managua January 26-31, 1981. It was published in the February 1, 1981, issue of Barricada, *the FSLN daily. The translation is by* Intercontinental Press.

Compañeros of the presiding committee of this extraordinary gathering in solidarity with our people and our struggle;

Compañeros Julio López and Raúl Guerra;

Brothers and sisters from all those countries and peoples that for a long time have been supporting the formidable efforts of the Nicaraguan people to conquer their freedom, national independence, and social progress:

Today we would like to give you some general information on the achievements and the prospects of the Sandinista economy. We do so at a time when the reactionary forces of imperialism, along with the Somozaists and the reactionaries here at home, are bent on setting up obstacles to the Sandinista people's revolution.

That is why we think your presence here has a deep revolutionary significance — both of internationalism and of solidarity — because it amounts to a show of support from the whole world, from democratic peoples, from progressive and humanistic consciences, from those who have faith in the people's future. At the same time, it is an incentive for us Nicaraguans and revolutionaries to know that in the battles that await us in defense of our national sovereignty and independence, we can count on the tremendous strength of international solidarity.

We will not mention figures because we will be distributing documents and statistics that show the successes and obstacles of the Nicaraguan revolution in its economic and social development. We know that as you carry out your tasks of solidarity and support to the Nicaraguan cause you need to understand as we do the basic conditions, the favorable and unfavorable aspects of our economic and social development, and our current achievements and problems.

In looking at the basic conditions of the Sandinista economy, we must first take up the objective situation we found ourselves in when the revolution triumphed. First, a sparsely populated country with a little more than 2 million inhabitants concentrated in the area along the Pacific Coast. Fifty percent of the population lives in the countryside, and 50 percent in urban areas. With the exception of Managua and five or six cities with 30,000 or 40,000 inhabitants, the latter are practically all small peasant villages. So, much of the 50 percent of the population called urban is actually a rural population as well.

There are some 800,000 workers incorporated into the economic activity of the country; of these, more than 60 percent were illiterate. So the labor force was a poorly skilled one, mainly engaged in handicrafts and peddling in the towns. In the countryside, tenant farmers cultivate basic grains on tiny plots, while the bulk of the agricultural labor force works picking cotton and coffee and cutting sugarcane.

We have had an economy in which development has been slight, where alongside a relatively small industrial sector we find a very broad range of handicrafts. In the countryside, export-oriented latifundia are complemented by a very extensive sector of small peasant production.

The main features of the Nicaraguan economy are economic backwardness, dependence on imperialism, and a predominantly capitalist socioeconomic structure, in which we nonetheless find many who subsist on precapitalist forms of production, both in the urban handicrafts and peasant sectors.

We have a highly developed infrastructure in the Pacific zone, while in the central and Atlantic zones the conditions for production, transportation, and communications are almost totally lacking. The Atlantic Coast has more than 60,000 square kilometers but only 200,000 inhabitants. That is, an area three times as large as El Salvador but with a population thirty times smaller.

So the objective economic conditions the Nicaraguan revolution was faced with were a backward structure, cultural oppression of the workers (the majority of the population), underdevelopment, and economic dependence.

As is well known, Nicaragua is a country that produces enough food for its own people and has a quite efficient peasant economy. But it must also be taken into account that the economic power of capitalism was mainly brought to bear on agricultural exports, with the aim of meeting the requirements of the international capitalist market. This forced a weak and stagnant natural economy to serve as the basis of imported technology so as to meet the needs of a dynamic agricultural export sector.

We are dependent not only because of what we export to the international capitalist market but also because of what we must import — machinery, materials, technology, and capital — in order to produce.

Owing to the rapid development of certain sectors of our economy, such as agriculture, without a corresponding development of industry, we are forced to buy all our machinery and technology abroad. This prevented our traditional handicrafts from being transformed into a national industry.

The warriors of the past century were unable to build the cotton gins, coffee processing plants, or sugar mills that later would proliferate in the country. Those artisans who manufactured twine, domestic goods, bowls, or carts were unable to become manufacturers of often highly sophisticated pesticides and fertilizers overnight.

Therefore, when the Sandinista revolution triumphed on July 19, our underdevelopment and dependence were of what we term the "qualitative" type, meaning the enormous difficulty of achieving independence in culture, technology, and industry, in order to become independent in agriculture.

This may sound somewhat dramatic but it is a reality which exists not only in Nicaragua but also in many countries of the so-called Third World.

Therefore, making a revolution in disadvantageous conditions meant in itself drawing up a long-term strategic program aimed at striking at aspects of Nicaragua's economic and social problems that could be described as crucial — a program to strike at backwardness, to strike at underdevelopment, to strike at economic dependence.

Thus, our revolution put forth a program that might be called the program of a poor country, of a small, backward country which has to work for its national independence, which has to work for its economic independence, which has to work for the cultural betterment of its illiterate work force, which has to develop vast areas in the country where our backwardness is total, which has to redress the demographic and economic imbalances existing in our territory, where the contradictions of neocolonialism, capitalism, and imperialism's oligarchic enterprises have coincided to create chaos and economic anarchy. That is what we found on July 19.

We are aware that the more backward a country is, the more difficult it is to achieve social progress. Precisely for that reason, we have not worked in a spectacular manner. We know that this is a very difficult task, because the country needs substantial investments for development. Much time is needed to master technology, much time is needed to lay the foundations of a sound, independent economy.

That is the strategic aim we are working toward with spirit and will. But that is the long-term challenge. On July 19 our immediate task was to provide the basic necessities of our people.

Economic doctrines and romantic ideas are no good if the people are hungry. And on July 19, in addition to terrible material destruction, we found a quite onerous foreign debt. At the same time, there were the aftereffects of a capital drain of more than $800 million.

There was, of course, the basic economic and social conditions we found: backwardness, underdevelopment, poverty. We found a country that was totally bankrupt, with no foreign currency, no foreign savings; with a debt of $1.6 billion, and destruction amounting to more than $800 million, which affected more than 35 percent of the industrial production and more than 25 percent of agriculture.

The war coincided with the harvest of basic crops and, some time later, the cotton harvest. So in 1979 and part of 1980, those basic crops were lacking. The basic diet of Nicaraguans consists of corn, rice, and beans, and it so happened that in that year there were no beans, rice, or corn.

And, worst of all, we would not be able to export cotton, the prime crop for Nicaragua's survival. Of the 320,000 *manzanas** traditionally sown, it was only possible to sow 50,000.

We had to devote a large amount of resources to the rehabilitation of the infrastructure. You know that Somoza's regime vented its rage on the factories, on strategic industries and production units.

Much was destroyed in the countryside also, where agricultural machinery was pillaged. Tobacco was virtually looted, and they took away more than $3 million worth of machinery. Destruction was general.

Our foremost job at the time was the rehabilitation of the infrastructure, and to this end we had to spend large sums of foreign currency. Our debts increased because we had to buy spare parts and equipment in order to return to relative normalcy.

In Nicaragua, normalcy has depended to a great extent on foreign credit. If there is transportation, it is because we have used credit lines abroad. If the factories are running, it is because we have brought in a considerable number of spare parts, which has meant great expenditures in foreign currency or external loans. If we have worked success-

*1 manzana = 1.726 acres

fully in economic reactivation, it has been at the expense of growing foreign indebtedness.

The first six months of the revolution were dedicated to administrative organization, to extirpating the whole corrupt cancer of Somozaism. This meant incorporating into state and economic management a politically, administratively, and technically inexperienced intelligentsia. It meant organizing the revolution's ranks, creating large mass organizations and an army truly capable of facing any attack by Somozaism and reactionary forces abroad.

So the 1980 program was called the Plan for Economic Reactivation. This program called for using the country's productive forces to the utmost while making substantial investments in material, human, and financial resources. The latter made it possible to put the productive machinery back into motion, under the difficult conditions our country found itself in.

We have been talking about objective socioeconomic conditions; that is, the legacy of the past, the legacy of backwardness, underdevelopment, and poverty. That is the most difficult thing we face. We have been talking about the legacy of destruction caused by the war, the collapse that occurred with the revolution and its aftermath, and the cost to our country all this signified.

But there is a third aspect we want to emphasize so that the logic of the Sandinista economy can be fully understood. This aspect is the political one — the question of national unity.

We seek to emerge from poverty and underdevelopment, to counter dependency, and to rehabilitate and reactivate our economy while maintaining national unity. It is a very difficult and complex task, one that might even seem to call for wizards or magicians. Sometimes the contradictions involved are so deep and irreconcilable that it is difficult for us to harmonize them.

How can we deliver our people from poverty, while at the same time reactivating our economy and utilizing all our productive forces? And how can we do this while large sectors of our economy are still subject to forms of exploitation that are characteristic of capitalism in underdeveloped countries?

In fact — and this is perhaps one of the deepest concerns of our revolution — the economic considerations of the Nicaraguan revolution are not as important to us as its political aspects.

In a way, the Nicaraguan revolution is not just a Nicaraguan one. It is a revolution made by a people who share the problems of many other peoples like our own — peoples who still live under the iron rule of military dictatorships, which as we all know are the typical and classic forms used by the imperialists to dominate our peoples.

The imperialists install such military dictatorships where they cannot intervene directly or where there are no local oligarchic or bourgeois classes with enough economic power and political talent to guarantee the subjugation of the people. So they turn those classes into their intermediaries, into representatives of their interests in such countries.

This is what they do when they cannot intervene directly — either because the people struggle as our people did in Sandino's time, or because international diplomatic considerations prevent them from doing so. (I think it would be difficult for the imperialists to intervene in a direct, military way in Colombia or Venezuela, for example.)

Here in Nicaragua neither the Liberals nor the Conservatives could guarantee imperialist domination. So when it became impossible to check the vigorous advance of Sandino they had to intervene — first directly and then by means of a military dictatorship that placed itself above all the classes and parties and represented imperialist interests exclusively.

Imperialism's military dictatorship — which also protected a servile, subsidiary, and irrelevant local form of exploitation — was destroyed by the Sandinista revolution. The typical and classic form the imperialists have introduced in Guatemala, El Salvador, Chile, and other Latin American countries suffered an important defeat here in Nicaragua.

This is why national unity is of such great importance to the Nicaraguan revolution.

Some months ago, a U.S. State Department official said that the pillars of what he called the "traditional regimes" were being torn down in Central America. Those pillars were in crisis, he said, explicitly pointing to the reactionary Church hierarchy, the oligarchy, and the fascist army. Those were the three pillars on which the so-called traditional domination rested.

According to this official, that is what had maintained the unity, stability, and cohesion of society. But what is now involved is that once this pattern was broken in Nicaragua, a new type of national unity appeared. Here there is stability, peace, and production.

We are not going to say that we are living in paradise, because there are contradictions and an intense ideological struggle. The reactionaries keenly desire to win over the middle strata of the population. They are making a stubborn effort to take advantage of the backwardness of the peasantry and the humble people to turn them against the revolution.

But one thing is certain: here, neither the reactionary hierarchy, the oligarchy, nor the military dictatorship can guarantee national unity any longer. There is unity, but under revolutionary rule. It is a unity rooted in the mass organizations, the organizations of the workers, peasants, students, and democratic women.

In other words, a people's unity with people's armed power, and a government program allowing for and stimulating the participation of all strata in the national reconstruction of Nicaragua. And all those factors are united under the firm guidance of our vanguard, the Sandinista National Liberation Front.

Five years ago that was a dream, an illusion. But now this State Department official realizes that while the old traditional patterns have been replaced by revolutionary patterns, peace, stability, and the smooth functioning of the economy are maintained. This is a victory of the revolution, this is a victory of all the revolutionaries in the world. And that is even more important than the specifically economic aspects.

Our main concern, therefore, is to fully use the nation's productive forces. And we think that under a revolutionary power it is also possible to induce the forces of the middle class and even the bourgeois sector to join us, in the same way an agricultural worker offers his energy, his sweat, his blood in the task of building the new homeland, which is what the peasants and workers are doing.

In order to strengthen the country's unity we can benefit from the bourgeoisie's experience in agriculture, from their management skills in industry. The contradictions arising from their participation are less significant than the solutions they provide for carrying on the struggle against the commmon enemy.

The contradictions inherent to social classes are less important than our material achievements in reconstructing the foundations of national economy, in the struggle for development, in the struggle against backwardness, and indeed in the struggle against economic dependence, because the rationale of the economy is centralized in a plan, in an economic program that assigns a role to each social force.

We are not referring to that old, backward economy where a big manufacturer could do as he pleased. In the first place, a big manufacturer has to contribute to the financial system and has to pay a fixed interest rate reimbursing the money that was lent to him by the state, by the people.

Secondly, when he produces, he has to pay production taxes, export duties, capital gains taxes, and real estate taxes, as well as income taxes, because our economy operates on this basis. And of course, there is our political capacity, the capacity to regulate what some call the reproduction of capital.

We nationalized foreign trade and the banks. This means that the state receives all the foreign currency. No big cotton producer here can obtain dollars, only córdobas. With those córdobas he has to pay bank interest, production taxes, export duties, capital levies, and income taxes.

Somewhere, usually in a bank, he will keep a rather significant amount. And that money is also available to be used by our economy as a whole.

Thus, we are also able to use these resources, these individuals, as workers in national reconstruction. Their contribution is significant.

There has been no need to expropriate the means of production. In reality, what we are expropriating are the surpluses.

We should seriously consider whether it is convenient or not for a poor, dependent, and backward country lacking a skilled work force to use these resources and exploit the land by introducing state and national control over the surplus rather than over the means of production themselves.

Of course, this is a very special circumstance in Nicaragua. It probably does not apply to other countries. But we do have control over property, profit, and surpluses.

The middle and upper strata feel that we respect their property, and that they can live somewhat affluently. They feel somewhat at ease, because we allow them the possibility of owning some of the means of production.

We believe that rather than being a problem for the revolution, this is vital for the revolution. Unity to confront imperialism is vital. That is why our economic program has included such elements of unity both in the 1980 plan and in the 1981 plan as well.

What have we achieved in recent months? At the beginning we had set ourselves a really high growth rate. We were going to grow by 23 percent. Of course, this figure has to be seen in terms of the very difficult year the Nicaraguan economy had suffered. In 1979, Nicaragua's gross national product equalled that of 1962.

We had gone back seventeen years, so from a certain point of view this 23 percent growth was not so difficult to achieve when resorting to all our forces and using all our financial resources.

It was difficult in the organizational conditions, because of the material damage we had suffered and also because of the shock and turmoil our people suffered, the geographical distribution of the population, and other social factors.

But we can say that we have practically attained that figure, and in some aspects we have surpassed it, especially in agriculture. The employment goal of 95,000 workers was 92 percent fulfilled; in 1980 we were able to create 82,000 new jobs. We succeeded in the economic reactivation of our main lines of production.

As for coffee, the harvest will surpass by 7 percent the figure planned for 1980. The lowest figure for cotton production in the 1980 program was surpassed, the highest being 170,000 manzanas planted, the lowest, 120,000 manzanas. We planted 140,000 manzanas, but in terms of yield we will practically equal the figure that could have been expected from the 170,000 manzana goal.

We planted more than 45 percent over the figure planned for rice and 20 percent more in tobacco. As for sugarcane, we surpassed the plan's goal by 25 percent.

We can say that we recorded the most important and biggest grain harvest in our country's history. We had rain, transportation and communications problems that considerably reduced the harvest, and storage problems that considerably cut production.

Nevertheless, in agricultural production, both for domestic consumption and exports, we can say that our people made a great effort to reactivate the economy. The agricultural workers, the students who harvested cotton and coffee, the whole people, all the sectors of our people in a joint effort were able to achieve the goals set for national reconstruction in order to give Nicaragua and the Nicaraguan revolution our first major economic success.

Industrial reactivation faced problems, not so much because of lack of resources, energy, vitality, ability, and administrative capacity, but mainly because the Central American Common Market underwent a crisis. Virtually all our industrial production for exports, that is, our most important domestic production, is oriented toward the Common Market. El Salvador had market problems, as did Costa Rica, Honduras, and Guatemala. And we have not been able to market some of our products yet.

We think that when the situation in El Salvador is resolved in favor of the revolutionaries we will occupy a more favorable position economically because El Salvador is one of our major markets.

We want to underscore one interesting aspect — economic reactivation got a little out of control in the sphere of services.

It was natural that because of the physical destruction in agriculture and industry, it was going to be difficult to reconstruct. So the work force, especially small farmers and workers, were reoriented toward the commercial sector. Trade grew excessively, by 140 percent. This is a distortion, a trend toward creating too large a tertiary sector that will have negative effects if we do not check it.

But in general, we can say that the 1980 program was a success. We do not face the same situation we had at the beginning, that of 1962. We are already at the level of 1978. That is really a remarkable achievement, which gives us hope and encouragement for the coming year.

Generally speaking, 1981 will likewise be a year of reactivation. We will put stress on savings and economic efficiency. But economic efficiency in what sense?

You can see clearly that there are new administrators and new workers who lack experience. Where there is destruction — let us say, in a factory — if you grant the administrator 1 million córdobas to produce 100 units, reality will prove under present physical, administrative, and organizational conditions that 1 million córdobas in that production center will probably produce only seventy units. That is the problem we have faced throughout agriculture and industry, although it seems to have hit us harder in agriculture.

We have dumped lots of money — again and again — into small production units that never before had had access to it. They were not able to manage their resources efficiently, so instead of producing forty units, they produced twenty. That is why we are now facing financial problems, and perhaps some inflation, since there are large sums of money with no counterpart in products.

The 1981 program is aimed at solving this problem by using different variables — assigning credits more rationally, granting credits to those who can produce efficiently.

Somewhat romantically, at one point we were even traveling in helicopters and giving out credits to peasants who lived in very remote areas. The credits virtually fell into their hands from the helicopter. But who was going to gather that production? By which roads, by which means of transporation?

The fact is that the produce, if there was any, remained there because that money was spent on salt, shoes, and clothing and not on production.

Such romantic errors are made in every revolution. They are just the counterproductive side of the generosity of revolutionists.

In agriculture the problem was more or less the same. Imagine all Somoza's agricultural enterprises and production centers — some

2,000 of them. When we took office at the Nicaraguan Institute of Agrarian Reform we did not even know where they all were. We sent nine or ten compañeros out to locate them. All we knew was that there were ten in one place, twenty in another; we did not know what they produced.

In early 1980 we were still counting cattle. There were no records; production indices were unknown, but people had to be fed. We had to produce milk and coffee, we had to raise cattle. Then the National Bank connected a pipeline to siphon money to the Nicaraguan Institute of Agrarian Reform. Otherwise it would have been impossible.

One compañero we sent to Matagalpa reported 149 estates with 10,000 workers — we had to pay wages and back wages, and the land had to be tilled. At that time we had no accountants; we had to buy things and write invoices on scrap paper.

In those early days inefficiency was unavoidable. The 1981 program tries to solve this problem as well.

We must try to make the system efficient by implementing inventories and accounting systems, controlling costs, programming financing and production, making inventories from the smallest item to the biggest industrial enterprise, keeping a record of all the costs, reducing unnecessary expenses, curtailing waste, and fighting against unproductive employment.

Efficiency is one of the principals of the 1981 program. It means that if we invest 100 córdobas, we must get 100 units; and not only 100, but even 120. Efficiency must be the guarantee of a healthy economy and of austerity in this country.

You know that in many economic aspects Nicaragua depends on resources from abroad. In order to produce cotton, we have to import fertilizers, pesticides, agricultural airplanes, plows, and cotton harvesters. In fact, we possess only the work force and the land for cultivating cotton in Nicaragua, but the rest — that is, the technology — must be imported.

Within the framework of such austerity, we have to plan our savings. We must conserve fertilizer and pesticides and plant pest-resistant varieties.

You also know that we depend completely on oil imports. Last year we spent some $200 million on oil, while our exports accounted for less than $500 million. This year we will have to spend $280 million dollars on petroleum alone.

Should this situation continue, by 1985 our exports will go only to buy oil. This situation is really unbearable, not only for Nicaragua but for all the poor economies that lack this resource.

We know that the oil-producing countries have a legitimate right to make those who have always exploited them pay. But the countries of the Third World account for scarcely 3 to 8 percent of world oil consumption, while current oil prices represent for Third World countries the cost of survival itself.

We could even say that oil prices are one of the most destabilizing factors, one of the most threatening and destructive factors for our economies.

The world has to do something about it. We have to do something about it. If a decision should be made to make the developed countries pay the oil bills of the underdeveloped countries, that would be completely just.

Oil prices for the developed countries should be increased according to consumption in the Third World. Third World countries should receive their oil free of charge or even be subsidized by the developed countries.

What we are suggesting is not out of the reach of those nations for a very simple reason. Some Third World countries like Brazil consume a large percentage of that oil, so excluding Brazil and other relatively large countries, we, the smaller countries, account for only 2 or 3 percent of world oil consumption.

So, if we charge to and demand from the developed countries this 3 percent, we could quite easily solve the problem of our economy. We think that this struggle — our struggle, the struggle of all the underdeveloped nations, and your own struggle as well — must be waged, because we have to make people aware of this problem.

This problem alone could destabilize us economically. The time will come when we will have to say "Energy or death!" at the same time we say "Free homeland or death!"

This is a problem we are facing now because we also have to pay our foreign debt. If we pay for oil and for our foreign debt, we will be producing only in order to import. This is a vicious circle.

We could say that this is the most acute and burning aspect of economic dependence. A country that exports at increasingly lower prices and imports at increasingly higher prices will always be indebted, increasingly indebted.

What has been the response of the international capitalist economy? To lend at high interest rates. They buy at low prices, they sell at high prices, and they lend us the deficit. So we face mounting indebtedness, a spiral that will finally force us to declare: "From now on we will not pay a single cent."

We only owe $1.6 billion. Some countries owe as much as $65 billion, and there are others that owe $20 billion, or ten, or three, or four. The time will come when an economy like Nicaragua's will be suffocated and there will be a collapse. At some point there will be a collapse.

We must all be aware of that. This applies both to the compañeros who are in a position to launch campaigns to familiarize public opinion with the situation, and to those representatives of friendly countries where perhaps there are still great shortcomings in terms of fully understanding the complex problems our revolution faces.

There are tremendous economic resources that could be mobilized for the strengthening of a revolutionary process like ours, if everyone were convinced that this revolution has a bearing, not only locally or regionally, but on the whole world.

This is an ongoing revolution in a Third World country that has been able to overthrow imperialist power, that is building national unity with a democratic and pluralistic orientation, that is working miracles in the midst of a series of contradictions, that is trying to make a contribution to our peoples so as to open to them the road to liberation. All this can make the vacillators in many places put confidence in the revolutionaries who are able to lead their nations towards real independence, social progress, and stability.

And each and every brother or sister in each and every country must work tirelessly so that solidarity and material support, economic and financial cooperation, might contribute to breaking through the economic and financial barriers that international reaction is setting up.

A few days ago they warned us that should the Nicaraguan government persist in alleged military aid to the revolutionary movement of El Salvador, the $75 million loan from the U.S. government would be immediately suspended, and that its payment would be immediately demanded.

They have now paused to review the granting of the remaining $15 million. We are morally and politically ready to resist these aggressions.

In any case, we will set a fresh example, an example for everyone. Perhaps it will be an example differing from Chile's simply because of disproving the notion that there cannot be a second revolution in America or that the revolution can be reversed. We think that when a revolution is a real one, it is irreversible.

So our example might well be that wherever imperialism seeks to reverse a revolution in Latin America, it will find a people ready to fight to the last drop of blood for their independence.

We consider these aspects to be really important. We know that our essential responsibility is to work for the building of the Nicaraguan economy, but it is still more essential to defend ourselves, to mobilize our people, to prepare an army capable of dealing blows to any other army. It is more essential to see that our mass organizations are armed to the teeth.

It might seem to be a contradiction that the defense of our economy, of economic independence, of the actual construction of a progressive economy seeking social justice should be based not only on an economic program, but also on the armed struggle against foreign aggressors.

Our economy might drop to 1940 levels. The circulation of vehicles might cease in this country. We might have immense difficulties with supplies. But we would be securing the future, while reaffirming the right of our country to act according to its interests.

That is why figures are not as important as the way in which we combine certain efforts. The important thing is revolutionary construction, the ability to make the revolution prevail, the ability to maintain national sovereignty and the rights of the Nicaraguan people, to rebuff imperialist financial, political, or military threats and not to yield to their pressures.

We are ready even to die in order to prove it once more — as we proved it during our struggle against the filibusters in 1856, as we proved it during the 1926-33 war, as we proved it on July 19 — and this time with more capacity, ability, experience, self-assurance, and weapons. Nicaragua can be swept away, its land destroyed and turned into salt and ashes, but it will never be conquered.

Great efforts have been made in the cotton harvest, which lacked manpower this year, as we had foreseen. We would like to invite you, once you have completed your program, to pick cotton for Nicaragua.

I intended to give you a brief report, but it turned out to be a speech. In concluding, I would like to thank you on behalf of our people and government for your encouraging presence. We are also pleased to note the presence of dearly beloved brothers and sisters who all for many years have been supporting the worldwide struggle for Nicaragua.

We would like your stay to be very fruitful, and we are going to make all possible efforts for you to draw the highest benefits from this historic and excellent meeting of solidarity with the Nicaraguan people.

Thank you, compañeros.

The Second Anniversary of the Sandinista Revolution

by Tomás Borge

This speech was given before a crowd of half a million, gathered in Managua July 19, 1981, to celebrate the second anniversary of the Nicaraguan revolution. It appeared in the July 20, 1981, issue of Barricada. *The translation is by* Intercontinental Press.

Compañeros of the National Directorate of the Sandinista National Liberation Front;

Compañeros of the Government of National Reconstruction;

Special guests;

Heroic people of Nicaragua:

There is an immense multitude gathered here today — not to speak of the hundreds of thousands of Nicaraguans who couldn't make it to this plaza for lack of transportation.

We should pay warm and heartfelt tribute to the discipline and heroism of our people. Since two o'clock this morning, endless streams of men and women have been pouring towards the July 19 Plaza along all the highways.

We should also take note of the sacrifice and heroism of the 30,000 Nicaraguans, members of the mass organizations and the armed forces, who are standing watch on the four sides of the city.

They can't be here for this rally. They can't even watch it on television. But they undoubtedly share the excitement and happiness all of you feel at seeing the hundreds of thousands of Nicaraguans who have come here to support the revolution and the measures it has taken.

And this immense crowd has also come to pay tribute, not to those of us who survived the struggle and have the good fortune to be able to see the glorious victory, but to those who died, those who shed their blood to make this wonderful anniversary possible.

And what do these two anniversaries mean? In both cases it means the beginning of a new stage. The people who began this struggle never thought about the honors they might receive on a day like today.

They only thought about the urgency of their revolutionary duty

But they would not have been astonished at the idea of this huge rally, because they always had faith in the future, an unshakable confidence in victory.

In July 1961, fellow Nicaraguans, a course was begun that broke like a storm in July 1979. July 1961 is the first glimmer of a new idea that was justified and realized in July 1979.

Both dates fulfill the promise Sandino made when he said "I swear before our homeland and before history that my sword will defend the national honor and that it will mean victory for the oppressed."

In July 1961, the sword of Sandino was unsheathed, and in July 1979 the promise about victory for the oppressed was kept.

This sword is still unsheathed for cutting off the heads of the revolution's enemies.

Twenty years ago, when a group of people returned to Sandino's road of struggle, they did not foresee the magnitude the revolution would assume. Now the present generations understand what this process means, but it will take future generations to comprehend fully the heroism of the founders. Future generations will be the ones to understand the sacrifice, the courage, and the strength of past generations, and of the current generation of Nicaraguans.

When the Sandinista National Liberation Front was founded, the exploiting classes represented by the Somoza dynasty had closed off all possibility of a peaceful struggle. The time had come to take up once again the rifles of Sandino. Some people had already done it: the proud old white-bearded Raudales, Díaz, the journalist Sotelo, a farmer named Carlos Haslam, and many others.

The FSLN was, in the last analysis, the coming together of individual guerrilla fighters of that era. It was a union of different ideological and political ideas. It was a synthesis, as we have said before, of a whole history of heroic struggles, which began in the colonial period and broke like lightning bolts in the new epoch that opened up in 1821, which lying historians falsely call independence.

Don't worry, we are not going to tell the history of Nicaragua here, not even in broad outline. The history of our people, which is often distorted or unknown, is a heroic one. We just want to point out that July 1961 was the beginning of a definitive effort to take on not only the bloody dictatorship but also to break in a million pieces the heavy chains that tied us to Yankee imperialism.

The conditions under which the FSLN was founded were incredibly difficult and painful. They never stopped being difficult and painful. These were hardships and pain that our whole people was going through. What was special about those founders, who were considered mistaken and even crazy at the time, was that they had a sense of history. That they never gave up in the face of hardships and danger. That they started with nothing, with no money, no arms, no experience, no reputation.

What set them apart was that they had boundless faith in the people, that they were aggressive, brave, endlessly patient, and absolutely sure they would win in the end. They were in the first crop, when there were very few people doing the planting. They accepted the risk of death, when there was no possibility of actually seeing the new day in the immediate future.

They made the birth of the vanguard possible, they made the birth of the Sandinista National Liberation Front possible.

And obviously when we talk about the FSLN, we are not talking about something that is just a political party. We're not talking simply about an armed organization. We are talking about a historic response. We are talking about the indivisible reality of the FSLN and the Nicaraguan people.

As long as this people is militant and proud, as long as this people is made up of heroic workers, as long as the workers and peasants and all revolutionaries are ready to defend the national sovereignty arms in hand, as long as there are Nicaraguans who love the land where they were born, as long as this people exists, the FSLN will continue to exist.

For this reason, all the efforts of those who were born in Nicaragua but now want to go back to the past, of the bootlickers of the Yankees, will fail. They will never be able to separate the people from their vanguard.

For the same reason, when the masses express their desires — and also their dissatisfactions — the FSLN, which is their highest form of organization, makes these desires and dissatisfactions its own, makes them part of its revolutionary action.

That's why we say that the measures Daniel [Ortega] announced today were not pulled out of a magician's hat, but instead were the result of your struggle, the struggle of the great popular masses.*

The masses put forward their demands. The FSLN processes and synthesizes these demands and returns them in the form of concrete

*These measures strengthened the laws against decapitalization, authorized the confiscation of properties of Nicaraguans out of the country for six months, authorized the confiscation of large estates left idle or underutilized, and strengthened government controls on foreign trade. They were adopted by popular acclamation.

tasks that the masses, using their inexhaustible creative capacity, put into practice.

And when we talk about the masses, we are not talking about some vague accumulation of individuals, but rather of a consciously organized population. It is impossible to build up your revolutionary power without both the quantitative and qualitative development of the popular organizations. Unless the working class generates and carries through these changes, the revolution will stagnate and rot. In other words, it will stop being a revolution.

The masses themselves must always — now and in the future — speak up in a loud, clear voice on their own behalf. They must develop ways of participating and taking initiatives. The FSLN knows that the Nicaraguan people fortunately are not the mindless herd that the enemies of the revolution have tried to portray them as.

The sons and daughters of this country are not robots, not mannequins. This is a population every day more conscious, more audacious, and more creative. With this heroic population, we will make it to our goal, we will go all the way. With this heroic population that understands the world around it more clearly every day, it will be easier to come up with the right answers to the questions the revolution poses.

If the leaders of this revolution want to resolve the enormous and complicated economic problems that Daniel talked about, the problems of defense, of health, of education, then we will have to turn to the masses, to make ourselves one with the masses. There are no mathematical formulas or brilliant theories we can use to solve the problems that present themselves as the revolution unfolds. There is only one answer, only one response — the impressive power of the masses, free from bureaucratic shackles, devoting themselves to the daily tasks of rebuilding the country.

And the whole world, both our friends and our enemies, knows what this heroic people is capable of. Sandino was the one who showed the way in defending our national honor. And who were Sandino's followers? The same people who made this revolution, who are now making concessions to the classes that were finally thrown out of power in Nicaragua, after ruling for centuries.

And these are real concessions besides. For example, the businessmen have been given incentives to produce, and it was correct for this to be done. They were given all kinds of help and access to financial credit, and they will continue to get help in order to produce. But everybody should know that as of July 19, the day of our victory, their access to political credit is closed off. That road is closed to them, because power is now in the hands of all the descendants of Sandino's rag-tag army, of the barefoot soldiers, of the revolutionaries, of those who hunger and thirst for a justice that has been denied them since the beginning of our history.

And we are going to defend this power with the slingshot of David, except that in this slingshot we have, not a pebble, but rifle and cannon rounds.

And the brand of these rifles and cannons is not important. Whatever label they have on them, wherever they come from, we don't have to explain to anybody where we got these weapons, these rifles, these cannons. They are to defend our revolution and our people.

And where is this slingshot of David? In other words, who is in control of these rifles, these cannons? The militia members in their numerous battalions, which are sufficient to defend our homeland. They have the same boldness and determination that Sandino did, but their arms are better than those of our legendary guerrilla, our General of Free Men. Now it is the people who have the cannons, it is the people who have the tanks, it is the people now who have the rifles. And anybody who wants to fight against Nicaragua has to fight against this historic people, against this heroic and brave people.

We hate war, and our National Directorate has repeated this many times. We haven't organized the defense of our revolution for the purpose of conquering neighboring territories — or distant ones for that matter. We have done it in order to win peace. Our friends and neighbors can rest assured that this revolution was made in order to defend the land of our birth.

You all saw how our soldiers, our police, our militia members, the fighters of the Ministry of the Interior, the students, all went out to pick cotton. And Jaime [Wheelock] tells us that they were the most efficient workers in the cotton harvest. These fighters went out and sweated in the fields. And that's natural, because we are in the sweat business, not the blood business. We would rather spill our sweat in the fields and factories than spill our blood in the trenches. But there should not be the slightest doubt that these same men and women who went out to clean up the cotton fields are equally prepared to clean out the counterrevolutionary rats wherever they show their faces in our country.

Our people have an aptitude for peace, but we also have an aptitude for defense. It is very important for the enemies of our revolution to understand this, and if they have forgotten, we'd be glad to remind them about our history. And if any of them think they are up against a weak and divided government, we want to make clear to them that this is the strongest and most united government Nicaragua has ever had. The leadership of this revolution is a strong and united leadership, strong because it is a government of the people, strong because the government has the arms, and strong because of the rightness of its power and the power of its rightness.

The whole world has its eyes on Nicaragua. Our friends and our enemies alike are watching us and respect us besides. Nicaragua has already ceased to be an unknown place on the world map. Yesterday, Modesto [Henry Ruiz] told us that when he was in Europe someone was trying to check out where Nicaragua was, and by chance a fly landed on the map, and they said, "that's Nicaragua." But Nicaragua is no longer unknown. Now it is part of the wave of revolutions in our era. It is a country with great moral authority, not only in Central America, not only in Latin America, but in the whole world. We are proud to be Nicaraguans. This revolution transcends national boundaries.

Our revolution has always been internationalist, ever since Sandino fought in the Segovias. There were internationalists from all over the world who fought alongside Sandino, men from Venezuela, Mexico, Peru. Another who fought alongside Sandino was the great hero of the Salvadoran people named Farabundo Martí.

It is not strange that we are internationalists, because this is something we got from Sandino. All the revolutionaries and all the peoples of Latin America especially know that our people's heart is with them, beats alongside theirs. Our heart goes out to Latin America, and we also know that Latin America's heart goes out to the Nicaraguan revolution. This does not mean that we export our revolution. It is enough — and we couldn't do otherwise — for us to export our example, the example of the courage, sensitivity, and determination of our people.

How could we not be upset about the injustices that are committed in different parts of the world? But we know that it is the people themselves of these countries who must make their revolutions, and we know that by advancing our revolution we are also helping our brothers and sisters in the rest of Latin America. We know what is resting on our revolution — not only the aspirations of our people, but also the hopes of all the dispossessed of Latin America. This carries with it enormous responsibility, because as we have said before and repeat today, our internationalism is primarily expressed in consolidating our own revolution, working selflessly day in and day out and training ourselves militarily to defend our homeland.

And this is a big responsibility, a very big responsibility, because it is extremely hard to transform a society. I'm not going to go over the destruction, the looting of Nicaragua. Our country will demand from us more effort, harder work, more sacrifice in the future. Carrying forward the revolutionary process is harder, much harder, than the war itself. Because it involves a war against the misery of the exploited classes, a war against the misery that the exploiting classes have converted into a fact of life.

So we see that while we're in the process of dealing with one problem, ten new ones come up. Sometimes we lose battles and sometimes we win battles in rebuilding the country. But of course what is important is the direction we are moving in, the meaning of what we are doing, and the things we accomplish. Our errors can be corrected, but what is lasting are the revolutionary transformations.

We are creating a new society in which an individual is not a piece of merchandise, a society in which there are no wolves and lambs, where men do not live off the exploitation of other men. We are struggling to create a society in which the workers are the fundamental power driving things forward, but in which other social sectors also play a role, always insofar as they identify with the interests of the country, with the interests of the great majority.

The measures the Government of National Reconstruction has announced today are a step forward in the process of transformation demanded by the working class. But it is not possible to move forward without cutting into the interests of the selfish classes. So nobody should be surprised that these sectors are attacking the revolution. Even if it is true that not everyone in these classes is trapped in the web of selfishness or completely possessed by the demon of prejudice, nevertheless it is a fact that a big part of them have no interest whatsoever in changing the rotten structures of the past. For this reason, the revolutionary measures that are being taken provoke fury and insecurity in some sections of the minority class. They say the mixed economy is dead, that there is no more political pluralism. We repeat what our brother Daniel said here today: the revolutionary process is going to continue moving forward. Honest and patriotic employers and businessmen not only have the right to join in the tasks of production, but they will have the support of the revolution in doing so. In the same sense, we can speak of political pluralism, a mixed economy, and national unity — but always within the framework established by the revolution, not against the revolution.

A mixed economy, pluralism, unity, not to wipe out or weaken the revolution, but to strengthen it. Not to destabilize, but to stabilize. Not to bad mouth the revolution and stab it in the back with disgusting lies, as is happening every day, but to criticize with respect for the truth.

This is the sense in which the revolution has put forward the strategy of a mixed economy, so that the gentlemen of the business community can produce, for their own benefit but also to contribute to raising production in the country. But what has happened? We have to repeat what our brother Daniel has said.

There are a few patriotic businessmen who have understood what the new rules of the game are, learned the new laws of political arithmetic, and have adopted an honest and constructive attitude. But there are many others, the unpatriotic businessmen, who have refused to pitch in with the tasks of wiping out backwardness and poverty and taking up the challenge our economic difficulties present.

They have had a hundred years of chances, historically speaking. And we have to admit that they have accomplished some things, but always to enrich themselves at the expense of the workers' sweat. Every drop of proletarian sweat, and sometimes every drop of blood, was transformed through the businessmen's famous efficiency into luxurious wealth, all of it destined for their strong boxes.

What have these unpatriotic elements done for Nicaragua? They made it into a rubbish heap, into a lake of blood, into a valley of tears. Because they didn't teach the people to read and write. Because they did nothing for the health of the people. Because they took this country, which because of its natural resources should by right have been a paradise, and kept it backward and miserably poor.

Now the top representatives of this unpatriotic bourgeoisie demand that we rebuild immediately what it took them a hundred years to destroy.

Who decapitalized the country? Who assassinated Sandino and celebrated in an orgy of champagne and blood? Who made fabulous deals with the tyranny? Who made contributions under the table to Somoza's election campaigns? ["The bourgeoisie," the crowd responds]

Who grabbed up the peasants' land and has kept the workers under the yoke of oppression? ["The bourgeoisie"]

Who called our wonderful literacy campaign indoctrination?

Who chimed in and still chimes in with the crude anticommunist campaigns of Somoza, Pinochet, Stroessner, and all the rest of the gorilla animal life of Latin America and the CIA? Who slandered the revolution and who abuses the mass organizations with disgusting epithets? ["The bourgeoisie"]

Who asks for advice and takes orders from the representatives of the empire, of the same empire that tried to enslave our country, sowing death, destruction, and humiliation? ["The bourgeoisie"]

It was not you workers and peasants. You weren't the ones who decapitalized the country. You weren't the ones who went and stood at the door of the American embassy to ask permission for what you were going to do. And if it wasn't you, then who is it, who was it, who has it always been? Who are the traitors, the capitulators, the false prophets? ["The bourgeoisie"]

Sure there are good administrators within the bourgeoisie, there's no doubt about that. Unfortunately — and this happens in every revolution — the big majority of the guerrillas who won the war were of worker and peasant background. They aren't administrators. They don't have masters degrees in economics. Many of them, like Germán Pomares, learned to read in the course of the struggle.

We should note that fortunately a certain number of intellectuals have thrown their lot in with the revolution, and now they are taking on some of the most difficult and complex areas of state administration. But it is still true that our revolution, like other revolutions, has a very big shortage of scientifically trained personnel. Within the bourgeoisie there are people who were trained in famous universities. But the contradiction is that the people who were in the trenches and in the mountains were not the gentlemen with the Harvard educations but the illiterate workers and peasants.

Could we put a competent businessman in charge of a strategic area? Sure we could, why not? But could we ever put in charge of a strategic area a businessman who literally hates the revolution? We'd rather give the job to — as Modesto would say — a country bumpkin, because at least he could learn the job over time and would be inclined to give his energy and his life to the revolution.

In the same sense in which we acknowledge that there are patriotic businessmen, we also recognize the support that technicians have given. Because a lot of them — at least within the context of the small number that exist in Nicaragua — have assumed a patriotic and exemplary stance.

Professionals and technicians can play a leading role in the wonderful task of constructing a beautiful future. Technicians should remember that their scientific training isn't worth anything if they lose their humanity and put their skills at the disposal of the enemies of our people.

As we've already said this morning, Nicaragua faces a difficult economic situation. I'm not going to go over again the destruction, the low level of planting in 1979, the brutal decapitalization — all of which has a lot of responsibility for this crisis. Another factor which must be considered is our objective dependency on our traditional markets. But there's another thing, and we should say it again, and that's the errors we have committed, especially as a result of our inexperience.

It has been said that politics is a distillation of economics. So it is not surprising that a lot of the political and ideological problems we face turn up in the area of production, distribution, and consumption.

In other words, economic policy is basically the problem of power, and in order to take on the enemies of our people in the area of power we have to learn to consciously control the economy. This applies to all of us, the leaders of the revolution and the government, but not just to us. More than anything else it applies to the workers.

We have to grow up. We have to get over the adolescent phase of our revolution, in order to establish control over the anarchic tendencies of the market economy to which we are still tied by a thousand invisible threads.

The mass organizations have to take on the duty of keeping watch over the economy and letting the government know about instances of decapitalization, in accord with the new law against decapitalization that was announced just now.

The information that is gathered must be serious and objective, to avoid any possibility of injustice or subjectivism. But — and I want to emphasize this in the name of the National Directorate — the working class especially must respond with responsibility and with unity to the challenges history has given us. Without responsibility and without working-class unity, everything is much more difficult and, we could say, impossible.

Absenteeism on the job and other forms of indiscipline objectively are antirevolutionary attitudes and in practice are decapitalization.

The Agrarian Reform Law must be seen in all its political dimensions. It was a measure of simple justice to turn the land over to the peasants. It is an agrarian reform law that benefits all the workers, not just the peasants, but immediately puts the peasants to work producing on idle lands, and rationalizes agricultural production.

We will eliminate the big landlords with this law, we will give the land to the peasants, we will improve the conditions of the small producer and also give guarantees to the medium producer because they also know how to be patriotic.

They also know they can help contribute to justice in the countryside. The happiness we get from this turning over of the land must be converted into organization, work, production.

Our revolution is carrying out a historic demand of the peasants, as Daniel said, and making a reality the happy dream of Pablo Ubeda, of Rigoberto Cruz, and Germán Pomares, who gave their blood exactly on the earth which today the revolution is giving to the dispossessed.

With the agrarian reform we feel in our hearts a joy similar to that written about in the Bible where it says "Let the sea and all the inhabitants contained in the world roar. Let the rivers applaud and be joined by the mountains in cries of joy," because the love of justice is not only a revolutionary sentiment, but also a sentiment deeply shared by the Christian people of Nicaragua.

And so we see that in our free Nicaragua there are hundreds of thousands of Christian revolutionaries, men and women who today rejoice over the news of the solution the Catholics have arrived at with the bishops. A solution based on dialogue and respect, that recognizes the principle of the right of revolutionary Catholics to work shoulder to shoulder with their people, in the construction of a new society. It gives us pleasure to see the maturity of the Church's leaders.

We were saying before that the errors will be rectified but that the revolutionary methods will remain. So let us talk a bit more of our errors, but not like in the confessional, where you receive absolution and then go on sinning.

Let us speak frankly before the people, as a healthy self-criticism, to correct errors, to rectify our course.

Something we must criticize, and Daniel has already mentioned this, but we want to talk about it a bit more: bureaucratism. We inherited more than destruction. We also inherited the destroyer, bureaucratism. Public functionaries in the past were educated with the conception that their special jobs were only marginal to political decisions.

But the public functionary is not only a specialist, but today must also make political decisions.

Unfortunately, there are a great many functionaries that don't take the approach of directly resolving problems by working directly with you, with the masses. The state apparatus must be simple, dynamic, efficient.

When we created the nationalized sector of the economy, when we began to make health care, education, and culture available to everyone, that was when the number of public employees began to increase, logically. However, I think that we have gone too far. We have not only increased the functions of public workers, but we have also increased the number, and now the bureaucracy is giving birth to more bureaucracy. And with more and more employees and functionaries the solution gets harder and harder. So begins the red tape. Everyone in a sea of red tape, memoranda, forms. I think that the bureaucracy grew so much that it would have done well to compete in the baseball leagues, because it was throwing us all so many curves, and I think that the bureaucrats would have won the championship besides.

Sure, many of our problems can't be resolved because of objective problems, for instance the lack of material resources; but there are problems that don't get solved because of a lack of imagination. We have seen some incredible things in this regard.

Like the doctors, who have to register at the university, with the Ministry of the Interior, the Ministry of Health, and I think also with the Public Registry of Persons.

Sometimes it takes three days and even thirty days to get your hands on a public document, thus wasting all that time. I even know of the case of a compañera, who went to ask for a leave of absence when she was seven months pregnant, and they told her to come back with a sworn statement that she was pregnant. The future mother said, look, compañero, I am completely certain that I am not just swollen up, that I don't have dropsy.

I think it is an unpostponable obligation to confront bureaucratism. But how do we do it? By linking ourselves to the masses. The administrative leaders in the government at all levels must go to the heart of the problems, where the conflicts are, must get to know the procedures, get out of their offices, and simplify things. And if the leaders do this, so must the workers.

We must also combat another vice we have inherited from the past — converting the easy into the difficult. Of course, we are not against administrative controls. We are against uselessness, as we are against insolence and the bad manners with which our citizens are sometimes greeted in public offices when they go for information or service. Yes, in Somoza's time the haughty dominated, the arrogant, but now what we must have is simplicity, courtesy, and Sandinista respect.

On the other hand, I think we have been soft on the functionaries who have abused their trust. We are already planning, as Commander Ortega said here, a law to deal harshly with those who rob the public treasury, above all with those who are corrupt, who have stolen the people's resources.

It is certain that we still don't have sufficient controls, and the controller general has undertaken major efforts to detect crimes against the public treasury, but it is now time to deal sharply with those criminals, who are the worst criminals, because they are not just robbing their neighbor, they are robbing the entire people.

For sure, the law that Daniel mentioned will have to be a draconian law, that can send criminals to prison for a long time, including up to the maximum. Jail those who rob even if it's only a pin.

We still have compañeros in the armed forces and in other sectors and other organisms, although fortunately very few, who think that the uniform or the responsibility the revolution has given them puts them in the category of special citizen who can ignore traffic laws, not stand in line at the movies, give or receive recommendations, make scenes in clubs and amusement spots.

These compañeros either will correct their behavior or will forfeit the right to be known as Sandinistas.

We have spoken of austerity, but in many institutions so far it's just rhetoric. There are innumerable abuses, squandering of gasoline, which means squandering our foreign exchange earnings. Of course, for instance, we have the right to have a good time, to have our parties. If we want to have a party we have it, there's no problem; but it must be put on with the simplicity and the prudence our poverty demands, the prudence demanded by our current problems and above all our revolutionary qualities.

In our offices we must economize on the use of paper, electricity, economize in every way possible. In every way possible, except work, effort, and sacrifice. Austerity must be for everybody, not just for the workers in the fields and in the cities, upon whom the weight of our economic difficulties has fallen up to now.

War to the death, then, against bureaucracy, free spending, pilferage, corruption, and abuses. Let us put an end to these evils, in order to give land to the peasants, to make the revolution, honor the memory of those who died, to end theft, crime, and corruption. That's what those generous, brave, and humble men we recall with such profound respect today gave their lives for. And how could we fail to recall our heroes? How could we fail to recall them on this glorious occasion? How can we not sense the eternal presence of Santos López, veteran fighter of Sandino's army, who, carrying with him the weight of the years, still had in his eyes the old gleam from the jungles of Segovia?

How could we fail to recall the indefatigable Faustino Ruiz, of whom it was once said that he never said a word that wasn't on the mark like an arrow in the heart? How could we fail to recall Jorge Navarro, who carried a knapsack full of joy, and a handful of grenades? How could we fail to recall Rigoberto Cruz, Pablo Ubeda, first in the hearts of the peasants? Francisco Buitrago, a student who knew many things, but never knew fatigue or dismay? How could we fail to recall, how could we fail to have a deeply felt remembrance of Germán Pomares, that intrepid forger of the dawn? Or José Benito Escobar, that worker whose trades were gunpowder and the people? How could we fail to recall Silvio Mayorga, who created a gentleness that was always at the side of every Sandinista? How could we fail to recall, with our hearts full of

Nicaragua, Carlos Fonseca, the firebrand lighting up the night?

It is right that we remember them. It is right that our people repeat, in the mountains and in the valleys, the names of these heroes. Let the animals in the jungle, the fishes in the rivers, hear them. Let their bombs burst like flowers on the faces of the children, so that their sacrifices may find an echo in the consciousness of the humble, of the exploited, whom they held so dear in their hearts. They and those who followed in their footsteps made possible the return of the flags and the return of hope. They made possible this revolution of rifles and guitars, of audacious poems, of free peasants, of free workers, of a free people who took into their own hands for all time the reins of their historic destiny.

Honor and glory to these simple sons of our people, covered today with the respected and heroic black and red flag of the FSLN. With the same flag that rescued the blue and white flag of our homeland, which once was sold out by the traitors to their people. The blue and white flag, defended by the black and red, today wave sure of themselves, and with legitimate pride in the middle of this violent rebirth, of anthems shouted in combat, of a generous and heroic people that at last is master of the sun, the rain, and the earth, where the bones of its heroes and dear martyrs are buried.

For those two flags: the flag of our homeland and the black and red flag of the FSLN, let us shout, Nicaraguans: Long live the FSLN! Long live the immortal pioneers of our revolution! Long live the second anniversary of our victory! Long live the agrarian reform! Long live free Nicaragua!

Patria Libre!

[*"O Morir!"* the crowd responds.]

An Appeal for Justice and Peace

by Daniel Ortega

This speech was delivered to the General Assembly of the United Nations on October 7, 1981. It was printed in English in the UN's Provisional Verbatim Record of the Twenty-Ninth Meeting. *Minor stylistic changes have been made for consistency and readability.*

The death of the president of Egypt, Anwar el-Sadat, is another tragic event that once again brings to the forefront the urgent need to contribute to the quest for a real solution to the Middle East question which once and for all will put an end to the violence that besets the fraternal peoples of the Arab world.

Humanity is living through a crucial moment in its history as a result of the great tensions that today more than ever threaten peace. Nicaragua has deemed it timely and necessary to bring to this assembly, among other things, a number of specific proposals capable of contributing to the cause of peace in the world.

We are today the bearers of a specific proposal in our search for a rational way out of the profound crisis affecting the Central American area, the most critical point of which is El Salvador. This is the main reason for our presence in this assembly, where we are certain we shall meet with the favorable reception warranted by the serious circumstances of the moment.

We are the bearers of a specific proposal aimed at assisting Central America in its struggle for peace, at the very moment when that peace is disrupted by the escalation of the arms race in the world, with billions of dollars being invested in the production and emplacement of medium-range missiles, rockets, neutron bombs, and so on; at the very moment when the progress achieved on strategic arms limitation agreements (SALT II) is being seriously jeopardized by the hegemonistic policy of the present United States government.

We are the bearers of a specific proposal aimed at assisting Central America in its struggle for peace, at a time when the racist regime in South Africa is invading Angola, promoting destabilizing actions in Zambia, invading the southern part of Mozambique, and training mercenaries to invade Zimbabwe, all of this with the support of the present United States government; at a time when Libya is the victim of acts of aggression deriving from United States policy which have even led to two aircraft of the Libyan Air Force being shot down over its own territorial space in the Gulf of Sidra.

We are the bearers of a specific proposal aimed at contributing to the cause of peace in Central America at a time when the government of Israel, with the full support of the United States, is carrying out acts of terrorism against the Palestinian people, and against the Lebanese people, murdering hundreds of people, as well as bombing the Tammuz nuclear research center in Iraq.

We are the bearers of a specific proposal aimed at contributing to the cause of peace in Central America, at a time when there is an increase in spying flights by United States aircraft in the air space of Democratic Korea and the economic blockade and political and military threats against Cuba, and the occupation of Guantánamo, continue; at a time when the people of Grenada are harassed and attacked; at a time when the implementation of the treaties concerning the Panama Canal Zone, for which Gen. Omar Torrijos fought and died, is placed in jeopardy; at a time when resolutions of the United Nations concerning the independence of Namibia are flouted.

We bring a specific proposal aimed at assisting Central America in its struggle for peace, at a time when the enemies of peace brandish philosophical concepts to justify their warlike nature, while at the same time perpetrating acts of aggression.

That is why today we also wish to contribute to the cause of peace by condemning the South African regime, expressing our solidarity with the peoples attacked by that regime, expressing our solidarity with the patriots of the South West Africa People's Organisation (SWAPO) as the sole legitimate representatives of Namibia; supporting the frontline states; expressing our support and solidarity with Libya and with the Palestine Liberation Organization (PLO), the sole representative of the Palestinian people; with the people and government of Democratic Korea; with the people and government of Grenada; with the courageous, united, and strong people and government of revolutionary Cuba; with the struggle of the Polisario Front; with the resolutions adopted on August 20, 1981, on the implementation of the Declaration on the Granting of Independence to Colonial Countries and Peoples, wherein the inalienable right of the people of Puerto Rico to self-determination and independence is reaffirmed; with the people and government of Panama; with the people and government of heroic Vietnam, while repudiating the policy of punishment, and the threat and use of force against that people; with the coastal states of the Indian Ocean which are continuing their struggle to have that area declared a zone of peace and to obtain the consequential withdrawal of the different military fleets moving in the area. We also appeal to the fraternal peoples and governments of Iran and Iraq to seek a solution in the spirit of the Nonaligned movement, to the differences or claims that may exist between those two states.

Finally, may we once again express our solidarity with the people and government of Cyprus, with the people of Chile, with the people of Uruguay, and with the heroic people of Guatemala. May we also hail as a victory for peace the independence of the people of Belize and its membership in this organization.

We bring a specific proposal aimed at strengthening the worldwide efforts to ensure peace which Central America is today obliged to make at a time when that peace is also threatened by restrictive economic measures which make their full weight felt in the Third World countries, historically exploited by the developed countries.

The latest decisions on the subject made public by the government of the United States are clear proof of what we have just stated. The secretary of the treasury of the present United States government has said that the government intends to limit loans and credits to developing countries through the International Monetary Fund and the International Bank for Reconstruction and Development; and President Reagan himself, at the annual meeting of the International Monetary Fund and the International Bank for Reconstruction and Development, confirmed that decision, saying that for the poor countries there the only magic formula is that of the free market, a "magic formula" which has served only to make our countries poorer.

Despite the efforts made by the Third World countries to restructure their foreign debt and, by means of great sacrifices, to pay the servicing costs, the economic horizon is now so bleak that it compels us to serious reflection. Unless formulas in keeping with the economic realities of our countries are devised, there will be no way out except to cancel the entire foreign debt and its servicing costs, or the time will come when by common agreement we, the poor countries of the world, will have to say that we are not going to pay, because we cannot pay, because we have nothing to pay with.

We must not forget that in foreign debt servicing alone the developing countries must pay with blood and sweat more than $40 billion a year, without the least possibility of finding a solution to their economic problems. On the contrary, the situation is becoming more and more serious.

Who can overlook the fact that the price of products that we export declines all the time while the costs of production of those products increase because the spare parts, machinery, equipment, and so on become more expensive each day?

In 1977 our countries had to produce 338 bushels of cotton, 1,394 bushels of sugar, or 98 bushels of coffee to buy one tractor. Four years later, in 1981, we must produce 476 bushels of cotton — an increase of 41 percent — to buy one tractor; or 2,143 bushels of sugar — an increase of 54 percent or more; or 248 bushels of coffee — an increase of 145 percent. This is because the wealthy countries lend us money on hard items, sell more expensively each day, but buy each day at a lower price.

As a result of these unfair international terms of trade and of the profound injustices engendered by exploitation, a dramatic social, economic, and political crisis shakes Central America today. That crisis stems from the depths of the poverty of 20 million Central American men and women. In 1979 one in two 15-year-old Central Americans was illiterate. One out of eight children dies before the age of one. Three out of every ten Central Americans looking for employment do not find it. Twelve million men live without proper housing. For every dollar obtained by a poor Central American a rich man receives $48. According to recent studies by the Economic Commission for Latin America (ECLA), 8.5 million Central Americans live in conditions of extreme poverty.

It is there, in the old reality of the exploitation of the Central American countries and in the injustice with which the developed world treats our peoples, that we must seek the causes of the political and social unrest that is today shaking Central America — not in the Nicaraguan revolution, which is the first great historic attempt in Central America to eliminate the roots of the crisis.

The accusation leveled at the Sandinista people's revolution that it is the cause of rebellion in Central America lays bare the hypocrisy of those who are truly responsible for the dramatic Central American situation. The main solution to the crisis in the region lies in recognizing that the crisis is the product of the exploitation to which the Central American countries have been subjected and in developing a set of measures in keeping with that reality.

Between 1973 and 1980 Central America's foreign debt increased by five times, and by the end of 1981 it will reach the unprecedented figure of $7 billion. That debt today represents 140 percent of our exports, when barely three years ago it amounted to 80 percent. It is an increasing burden placed on the shoulders of Central American workers, because the payment of interest to creditors means that each year a larger proportion of the region's exports must be earmarked for it.

The high rates of interest, which obey the fiscal and monetary policy of the United States, punish those who have less and reward those who have more. So long as this situation is not corrected there can be no solution to the Central American crisis.

To solve its own crisis the United States is applying a policy consisting of raising to unbelievable heights the cost of financial resources obtained by our countries. This logically leads to the export of the United States crisis to the poor countries. This year alone $1.2 billion has been drained out of Central America and has found highly rewarded refuge in the developed countries.

In the past three years alone the Central American countries have lost $1.23 billion, which was transferred to the developed countries, the United States in particular, because of the deterioration in the purchasing power of their exports. As long as this situation is not reversed how can our countries develop, how can that crisis be solved?

That deterioration in the terms of trade is a veritable tax on our exports levied by the developed countries. Those countries must therefore provide finance to compensate for that deterioration.

In two years — 1979 and 1980 — the Central American countries lost international reserves amounting to $1.18 billion. Where, then, are our countries to find the necessary resources to finance investments to promote their development? What is required is a massive flow of concessional resources to finance our strategic energy, transport, infrastructure, and industrial and agricultural production projects.

We demand justice as countries that have been impoverished by centuries of exploitation and by those unjust international economic relations, but the United States closes its ears. The forthcoming conference in Cancún has already begun to be affected by the refusal of the United States to deal with items that would truly make it possible to deal with the explosive situation in the economic order of the world today, and by its denying Cuba — which at present occupies the presidency of the Nonaligned movement — in a manner that we can only describe as infantile, the right to participate in that conference.

But Nicaragua is convinced that countries like Mexico, France, Austria, the United Republic of Tanzania, Algeria, India, and others will be the standard-bearers and spokesmen in our demands for a new international economic order.

We said that we were bringing from our region specific proposals aimed at contributing to the cause of peace. We have explained that

the fundamental causes of the crisis affecting our area are economic
and that they have been brought about by the unjust relations existing
in the present economic order and by the overexploitation to which our
peoples have been and are subjected by exploiting minorities which
serve like eunuchs the interests of international exploitation. If we understand this, we shall also understand why there was a revolution in
Nicaragua and why there is a revolutionary war in El Salvador and
another in Guatemala.

If we want to find a serious answer to the situation in Central America we shall have to stop invoking the specter of the East-West conflict,
which is used by those who try to reject any change in the region. And
we cannot disregard or ignore the fact that all this picture of brutal
economic exploitation has been defended throughout our history by
aggressive United States policy.

After the United States War of Independence, the model of a federal
democracy based on ideals of freedom which inspired the struggles of
Washington and Jefferson was also the model for the leaders of the independence struggles of Latin America; and in Central America the
liberal federal state headed by Gen. Francisco Morazán was the off-
spring of those principles of the American revolution.

But that dream was to die very soon. The emergence of the Monroe
Doctrine, America for the Americans, was to represent the aggressive
will of Yankee expansionism on the continent and from 1840 onwards
our peoples were no longer to benefit from the influence of those ideals
of democracy and freedom but rather to suffer interference, threats,
the imposition of treaties contradictory to the sovereignty of our countries, provocations and acts of war among neighboring states, blackmail with the presence of the United States fleet in our territorial waters, military interventions, the landing of marines, and the imposition of corrupt governments and one-sided economic treaties.

More than 784 acts hostile to the right of our countries to sovereignty have occurred on our continent since that time, and more than 100
of them since 1960.

Why were our countries insulted, invaded, and humiliated on more
than 200 occasions from 1840 to 1917? Under what pretexts, since at
the time there was not a single socialist state in the world and the tsar
ruled over all the Russias? Treaties and loans were imposed on us, we
were invaded, we were given the status of protectorates under that
same thesis of American national security, which was first called the
Monroe Doctrine and later the manifest destiny and later still the big-
stick or dollar diplomacy.

The expansion of frontiers, secure maritime routes, military bases in the Caribbean, bought governments, and docile governments — these were manifestations of a liberal ideal which had become barefaced expansionism.

How can we explain the numerous acts of aggression and interference and the landings that occurred between 1917 and 1954 in Latin America, when there was still no Cuban revolution and Cuba could not be accused of interference — accusations that were to be reserved for the future?

The United States did not take over Cuba and Puerto Rico in 1898 and impose the Platt Amendment to save Caribbean territories from the influence of the Soviet Union, since the latter was not yet in existence.

The United States did not land marines in Vera Cruz, Haiti, and Nicaragua, nor did it from 1903 onwards arm the most formidable naval force ever seen in Caribbean waters to resolve the East-West conflict to its own benefit. It was simply defending the interests of its territorial expansionism, the interests of its financiers and its bankers, of those business tycoons who were beginning to beset Latin America.

Today, October 7, 1981, the United States is beginning near the sovereign territory of Nicaragua military maneuvers called "Halcon Vista," with the participation of its own naval, land, and air forces together with military contingents from Honduras. At this time, as in 1855 when the filibuster William Walker landed on our shores at the head of a troop of southern mercenaries, our country is threatened by aggression on a scale higher than that which we have known so far. At this time, as in 1912 when our homeland was invaded by marines and defended by the patriots led by Gen. Benjamín Zeledón, the national hero, there are greater dangers of further invasions of Nicaragua, whether direct or indirect. At this time, as happened in 1927 when we were invaded by the marines, against which the army, headed by General Sandino, defended our national sovereignty and fought for six long years, there are new threats from the present United States administration. At this time it is necessary to remember the history of aggression against Central American countries throughout more than a century:

1855. The William Walker filibusters landed in Nicaragua with the purpose of annexing the whole of Central America to the southern states of the United States. Walker proclaimed himself president and restored slavery in Nicaragua. That same year, the colonels in active service, Kinneys and Fabens, proclaimed the independence of San Juan del Norte, a sovereign territory of Nicaragua.

1856. Through the Dellas-Claredin Treaty, the United States ceded to England the territory of Belize, which did not belong to it.

1860. The United States intervened for the first time in Panama, under the pretext of restoring order.

1867. The United States affirmed its ownership of Nicaragua through the Dickinson-Ayon Treaty, which gave it the right to build the interoceanic canal.

1896. United States military forces landed in Nicaragua, at the port of Corinto.

1899. More United States military forces landed on our territory, in San Juan del Norte and Bluefields.

1900. The United States imposed on Nicaragua and Costa Rica the Hay-Corea and Hay-Calvo treaties to acquire control over the canal route through the Central American isthmus.

1901. The marines landed in the Panama isthmus.

1903. The marines landed in Puerto Cortes, Honduras.

1904. The marines landed in Ancon and other points in Panama. That was the year when Theodore Roosevelt elaborated the "Roosevelt corollary" — or, rather, the big-stick policy.

1905. A further landing of marines in Puerto Cortes, Honduras.

1909. The United States intervened in Nicaragua to overthrow the government of Gen. José Santos Zelaya through the infamous "Knox note."

1910. The marines landed in Corinto, Nicaragua, and attacked our shores until they imposed their own oligarchic government.

1911. The United States again landed its marines in Corinto, Nicaragua; imposed presidents in Honduras and Nicaragua; and compelled Costa Rica and Nicaragua to accept onerous debt consolidations and new loans.

1912. The marines landed yet again in Honduras and the United States began its military occupation of Nicaragua which was to last until 1925.

1914. The United States imposed on Nicaragua the shameful Chamorro-Bryan Treaty, which divided our sovereign territory.

1918. The marines landed in Colón and Chiriqui, Panama.

1919. The marines occupied Honduran ports to intervene in the electoral process.

1920. The marines landed in Guatemala on the pretext of safeguarding the lives of North American citizens and protecting the legation.

1921. The marines occupied the region of Chorrera, Panama.

1924. The marines landed in Honduras and occupied Tegucigalpa, and other cities of the country.

1925. The marines landed in Honduras and Panama, in both cases to break workers' strikes.

1926. After leaving the country for many months, the marines returned to occupy Nicaragua. That military occupation was to last until 1933, when the Yankee troops were compelled to withdraw in the face of the heroic resistance of the army, headed by Sandino, defending our national sovereignty.

1930. The North American fruit companies promoted frontier wars and military uprisings, imposed presidents, and undermined the national sovereignty of Guatemala, Honduras, and Panama.

1954. The United States, through the Central Intelligence Agency (CIA), overthrew the government of Gen. Jacobo Arbenz in Guatemala.

1961. The United States military mission directed a coup against a civilian-military junta of a nationalistic character in El Salvador.

1964. United States troops in the Panama Canal Zone attacked a nationalist demonstration and murdered thirty Panamanians.

1960s. Early in the decade the United States also launched the abortive invasion of Cuba.

1972. The United States signed with Colombia the Saccio Vásquez Carrizosa Treaty, which was harmful to the interests of Nicaragua's sovereignty. In that same year United States forces were taken from the Panama Canal Zone to Managua to safeguard the stability of the Somoza regime after the earthquake that destroyed that city.

1978. The United States attempted to impose a mediation policy in Nicaragua to preserve the system and prevent the triumph of the Sandinista people's movement.

1979. The United States secretary of state, at the Seventeenth Meeting of Consultation of the Organization of American States, requested military intervention in Nicaragua to frustrate the Sandinista people's success. American helicopters landed in Costa Rica, in accordance with a plan to interfere in our war of liberation.

1981. The United States sent military advisers, military helicopters, and war matériel to El Salvador and Honduras. It cut loans to our country for development and for the purchase of food by $81.1 million. It allowed the training of former Somoza guards in military camps in the state of Florida. It ratified the Saccio Vásquez Carrizosa Treaty as an act of provocation against Nicaragua. And it began with Honduras the "Halcon Vista" military maneuvers.

Two days ago Col. Samuel Dickens, an American officer and a member of the Council of the Inter-American Defense Board, stated on arrival in Tegucigalpa that the "Halcon Vista" military maneuvers

were but a sample and that the United States was ready to give its
support to Honduras in a war against Nicaragua and to attack the people and the revolutionary government of Nicaragua.

His lack of respect did not stop there. He also attacked the government of Honduras because it proclaimed that it was neutral vis-à-vis
neighbors like Nicaragua and a guerrilla war such as that in El Salvador. He also attacked the governments of Mexico and France. All this
accompanied the arrival in Puerto Cortes on the Atlantic Coast of
Honduras of the United States amphibious vessel *Fort Snelling* with
500 marines, three patrol boats, a tugboat, and military matériel.
There also arrived at the same time at San Pedro de Sula, Honduras,
two observation aircraft of the United States Air Force coming from
the Panama Canal Zone.

What can we call all this?

The United States also tries to use Central American territory — as
it did in the 1960s to attack Cuba — to attack Nicaragua now.

Acts of aggression, interference, pressure, and blackmail never
cease. Respect for the sovereignty of our countries has never been obtained from the United States. The expansionist thinking of the last
century, the gunboat treaties, the big-stick policy, have emerged
again.

In the face of these facts and threats we cannot remain silent or inac-
tive, because history justifies our belief that we can be attacked again
and that the sovereignty we won once and for all by force of arms on
July 19, 1979, is in serious danger. Peace and stability in Central
America are seriously endangered. Is this the kind of history that will
repeat itself in Central America?

Our peoples are ready to respond as Sandino did to any attempt at
direct or indirect aggression, either in Nicaragua or in El Salvador.
We all know that the threat of invasion is directed first and foremost
against those two peoples.

Will that interventionist policy continue to be imposed on the will of
the people of the United States? Will the policy of sustaining, arming,
and defending in Central America such criminal regimes as those of
Ubico, Hernández, Martínez, and Somoza continue to be imposed? It
would appear so, according to the nostalgic words of a representative
of the United States who, on her passage through Peru, affirmed that
she would prefer Somoza in power in Nicaragua rather than the Sandinistas.

How far will economic aggression, hand in hand with military aggression, against Nicaragua go? Will the policy of interventionism in
Central America again be imposed with impunity? Will the United

States continue to promote a wrong-headed policy in Central America leading to an explosive regional crisis that will make worse an already difficult international situation?

We wish to state yet again our firm position on this question. We want peace, but not at the cost of freedom. We do not want war, but if war is waged against us we shall resist with a people's war. We believe that although the picture is somber, the outlook threatening, there is still time to stop the warmongers.

Central America demands changes; the revolutionaries, the Central American patriots, are promoting those changes, and the Central American peoples are ready to bring them about. The just war being waged by the heroic people of El Salvador demands a true solution, one that cannot be obtained through elections based on bloodshed, one that cannot be obtained through paramilitary groups, one that cannot be obtained through ever greater intervention by the United States, one that cannot be obtained through genocide.

It is for those reasons that, in our quest above all for a stabilizing solution in the area, the Sandinista government of Nicaragua applauds the declaration made recently by Mexico and France concerning the search for a political solution in El Salvador as a result of a dialogue between the belligerents.

We also welcome the resolution on the situation regarding human rights in El Salvador; and the possible ways and means of achieving a political solution adopted at the Sixty-Eighth Conference of the Parliamentary Union, which met in Havana September 15-24, 1981; the proposed resolution on Central America and the Caribbean put forward by the Socialist International, meeting in Paris in September 1981; and the final declaration of the meeting of Intellectuals for the Sovereignty of the Peoples of Our America, held in Havana September 4-8, which also relates to the struggle of the Salvadoran people.

We said that we were the bearers of a specific proposal aimed at assisting Central America in its struggle for peace in the world. That is why today we fulfill the duty demanded of us by historic circumstances and inform you, Mr. President, and the representatives of this assembly of the nations of the earth of the proposals conveyed to us by the Salvadoran patriots. But first we should like to say that there is among us, accompanying the delegation of Nicaragua, the president of the Revolutionary Democratic Front of El Salvador and member of the Joint Political Commission of the Farabundo Martí National Liberation Front and the Revolutionary Democratic Front, Comrade Guillermo Ungo.

The proposals are dated October 4, 1981, and addressed to Commander of the Revolution Daniel Ortega Saavedra, coordinator of the Junta of the Government of National Reconstruction of Nicaragua. They are as follows:

The Farabundo Martí National Liberation Front and the Revolutionary Democratic Front authorize you to convey to the United Nations General Assembly, at its Thirty-Sixth Session and to the peoples of the world, our proposals concerned with possible peace talks aimed at solving the crisis at present afflicting our country. The following is the text of our proposals:

The Farabundo Martí National Liberation Front and the Revolutionary Democratic Front address the international community and peoples of the world because they consider the United Nations to be the expression of the principles of peace, justice, and equality among states and peoples and therefore the appropriate forum in which to express the aspirations of the people of El Salvador and its representative organizations, FMLN and FDR.

May we first of all express our gratitude for the many expressions of solidarity with the struggle of our people we have received from governments, as well as from organizations and political, social, and religious personalities, throughout our struggle. We wish most especially to express our gratitude to the governments and peoples of Mexico and France for their solidarity, for they have recognized our organizations as representative political forces. May we also express our thanks for the comments and proposals of most of the countries of the international community in support of a political solution.

If today our people, directed by the Farabundo Martí National Liberation Front and the Revolutionary Democratic Front, are involved in armed struggle it is because regimes of oppression and repression have closed the peaceful channels for change, leaving recourse to armed struggle as the sole legitimate alternative to the people in its quest for liberation; that is, the exercise of the universal and constitutional right to resort to rebellion against unlawful and bloodthirsty authority.

Our war is therefore a just and necessary war to build peace and bring about equality among all Salvadorans.

However, what we want is peace and to achieve it we are proposing a political solution, the objective of which would be the end of war and the establishment of a new economic and political order that will ensure for all Salvadorans the enjoyment of their national rights as citizens and a life worthy of human beings.

All this supports our express will to open a dialogue with the civilian and military representatives to be designated by the junta through a process of peace talks.

We intend to base those peace talks, which reaffirm our commitment to seek and implement a political solution, on the basis of the following general principles:

First, they will be carried out between delegates appointed by the Farabundo Martí National Liberation Front and the Revolutionary Democratic Front and representatives of the government junta in El Salvador.

Secondly, they will be conducted in the presence of governments which, as witnesses, will contribute to the solution of the dispute.

Thirdly, they will be global in nature, encompassing the fundamental aspects of the conflict on the basis of an agenda to be drawn up by both sides.

Fourthly, the people of El Salvador must be informed of every development.

Fifthly, they will be opened without either of the two parties establishing prior conditions.

In an effort to ensure a basis that will bring about a political solution, the Farabundo Martí National Liberation Front and the Revolutionary Democratic Front express the will to discuss the following points:

(a) The definition of a new political, economic, and juridical order which will make possible and promote the full democratic participation of the various political, social, and economic sectors, especially the poorer ones. Elections will be an important element of the mechanism of participation and representation of the population.

(b) The restructuring of the armed forces on the basis of the officers and men of the present army who are not responsible for crimes of genocide against the people and the integration of the officers and men of the Farabundo Martí National Liberation Front.

Our fronts regard elections as a valid and necessary instrument for the expression of the will of the people, providing there are the necessary conditions and a climate that will enable our citizens to freely express their will. In El Salvador at present the electoral process does not fill those requirements since the repressive apparatus of the regime which murders trade union and political leaders and activists, persecutes the progressive elements of the Church, and is responsible for the physical elimination every day of dozens of citizens remains intact. Similarly, martial law and press censorship are still in force and there has been an escalation in the war against the people with the aid of weapons and advisers sent by the government of the United States.

A political solution is necessary for our people, for the stability of the region, for peace and security among nations. This means that governments must scrupulously respect the principle of noninterference in the internal affairs of other peoples. That is why we are directly addressing the government of the United States and asking it to cease its military intervention in El Salvador, since that intervention runs counter to the interests of the Salvadoran and American peoples and endangers peace and security in Central America.

Our proposal meets the claims for justice in accordance with the purest principles of international law, the interests of nations and peoples of the world, and the quest for a peaceful settlement of the causes of hotbeds of tension. In their efforts the Salvadoran people express their confidence in the understanding, participation, and support of the international community in the achievement of their right to peace, freedom, and independence.

The document is signed by the Unified Revolutionary Directorate of the Farabundo Martí National Liberation Front and the Executive Committee of the Revolutionary Democratic Front.

We are convinced that this appeal for justice, this appeal for peace, will be recognized by all those governments that are truly concerned with the fundamental rights of mankind.

In the name of the dead, in the name of the tortured, in the name of the illiterate, in the name of the hungry, in the name of the exploited, let this initiative not be in vain; let the forces of reason and love, the forces of peace, triumph once again over the irrational forces.

Index

Absenteeism, 136
Administrators, 135
Adventurism, 57-58, 61
Agrarian reform, 15, 16, 50, 136, 137
Agriculture, 114, 121. *See also* Coffee, Tobacco
Agüero, Carlos, 57
Aguero, Fernando, 41
Alday, Concepción, 83
Alliances, 58, 77, 78-79
Andean Pact, 49
Andrés Pérez, Carlos, 49
Angola, 141-42
Anticommunism, 134
Anti-Somozaist opposition, 32, 38, 54, 56
Arbenz, Jacobo, 28, 149
Arias, Arnulfo, 29
Armed struggle, 29, 30, 33, 56
—casualties in, 47
—center of, 39
—and guerrilla warfare, 58
—inspiration of, 35-36
—interruption of, 32, 34, 35
—organization of, 73
—and working class, 38
Arms race, 49, 141
Army, 21-22, 50, 53
Army for the Defense of National Sovereignty, 8, 27
Asylum, 14
Atlantic Coast, 19, 114
Austerity, 139
Ayón, Tomás, 26

Baltodano, Mónica, 83
Banks, 15, 25, 49, 120

Begging, 18
Belize, 46, 143, 147-48
Benjamín Zeledón Column, 75
Blacks, 19, 21
Borge, Tomás, 9, 85
Britain, 26
Browder, Earl, 31
Bureaucratism, 137, 138, 139

Camp David accords, 48
Canal, 26, 27, 28, 46, 148
Capital (Marx), 100
Capitalists, 23, 25, 30, 39, 95; and revolution, 119, 130, 133, 134; skills of, 135; and Somoza, 56; strength of, 40. *See also* Conservatives; Liberals
Capital punishment, 87
Carazo, Rodrigo, 49
Carlos Fonseca Northern Front, 60, 63, 69
Carter, Jimmy, 56-57
Castro, Fidel, 44, 49, 61n
Catholic bishops, 106
Cattle raising, 24
Censorship, 55, 56
Central American Common Market, 121
Central Intelligence Agency, 7, 8, 149
Chamorro, Emiliano, 27
Chamorro, Pedro Joaquín, 56, 60, 62
Chamorro-Bryan Treaty, 27, 28, 148
Christians, 106, 107, 109, 110
Church, 90, 109, 110
Clayton-Bulwer Treaty, 26
Coffee, 24, 120
Communist Party. *See* Nicaraguan Socialist Party

Conservatives, 27, 30, 41, 56, 118
Contreras, Eduardo, 57
Coolidge, Calvin, 43
Cooperatives, 16, 96
Copper, 24
Corruption, 18, 56, 99, 138
Costa Rica, 28
Cotton, 23-24, 116, 121
Coups, 14, 30, 32, 69
Credit, 16, 116, 122, 130
Cuba, 7, 43, 147; blockade of, 46, 142;
    CIA invasion of, 8, 28; inspiration
    of, 7, 9, 32, 54
Culture, 16, 17

Daycare, 20
Debts, 16. *See also* Foreign debt
Decapitalization, 95, 96, 129n, 134
Defense, 126, 131
Dellas-Claredin Treaty, 147-48
Democracy, 14, 97; in U.S., 21
Democratic Arab Sahraoui
    Republic, 46
Democratic Union of Liberation, 56
Díaz Sotelo, Manuel, 32-33
Dickinson-Ayon Treaty, 148
Disarmament, 49
Disease, 18, 25
Doctors, 138
Dominican Republic, 28
Drug use, 18, 99

Earthquake, 56
East Timor, 47
East-West conflict, 146, 147
Economic Commission for Latin
    America, 51
Economic crisis, 23, 56
Economic integration, 24
Economic planning, 15, 123
Economy, 51, 113, 114; development
    of, 115, 120; mixed, 95, 96, 113, 134
Education, 10, 16-17, 25
Eight-hour day, 18
El Chipote prison, 110
Elections, 14, 34, 39, 97. *See also*

Pluralism
Electrification, 15
El Naranjo, 75
El Salvador, 103, 125, 141, 150,
    151-52
Employment, 114, 121, 144
Epidemics, 18
Exiles, 14
Exports, 50, 114, 145
Expropriations, 14-15, 49. *See also*
    Nationalizations

Factories, 14-15
Farabundo Martí National
    Liberation Front, 152
Farmers, *See* Peasants
50 años de lucha sandinista (50 Years
    of Sandinista Struggle) (Ortega), 53
Filibusters, 26, 45, 147
Firings, 18
Food production, 24
Fonseca, Carlos, 9, 23, 54, 57, 58
Foreign debt, 50, 51, 116; of
    Central America, 144; of Third
    World, 124, 143
Foreign investors, 15, 24
Foreign policy, 20, 45
Foreign trade, 15, 20, 23, 120, 144
Freedom of religion, 20, 107
FSLN. *See* Sandinista National
    Liberation Front
Fuenteovejuna, 104
Functionaries, 137, 138

Gambling, 18
García Laviana, Gaspar, 62, 63, 106
Gold, 24
Government of National Reconstruc-
    tion, 44, 133
Grenada, 45, 142
Gross Domestic Product, 51
Group of Twelve, 56
Guatemala, 8, 28
Guerrilla warfare, 30, 32-33, 55, 63;
    and armed struggle, 58. *See also*
    Armed struggle

Gutiérrez, Panchito, 62

"Halcon Vista," 147, 149
Hanke, Lewis, 26-27
Harnecker, Marta, 53
Haslam, Carlos, 32-33
Hay-Calvo Treaty, 148
Hay-Corea Treaty, 148
Herdocia, Leonte, 98, 99
Herrera, Leticia, 83
Honduras, 148, 149, 150
Housing, 18, 144
Human rights, 14, 85, 151
Hunger, 25

Ideology, 29
Illiteracy, 8, 16, 114. *See also*
    Literacy campaign
Imperialism, 13-14, 19, 21, 23, 44,
    118. *See also* United States
Imports, 115
Indians, 64, 107
Industrialization, 15
Infant mortality, 8, 25
Insurrection (1977), 66, 68-69
Insurrectional strategy, 58, 59, 70,
    71, 77
Intellectuals, 16, 31, 135
Inter-American Human Rights
    Commission, 85
International Bank for Reconstruc-
    tion and Development, 143
Internationalism, 113, 132
International Monetary Fund, 143
Iran, 45
Israel, 48, 142

Jinotepe prison, 92
Judges, 99
Judicial system, 94

Kampuchea, 44, 45
Knox note, 27
Korea, 47, 142

Labor laws, 17, 18

Land, 9, 15, 16, 24, 136
Lane, Arthur Bliss, 27
Lang, Edgar, 86
La Prensa, 56, 97
Laws, 85-86, 99
Lawyers, 99
Lebrón, Lolita, 46
Legal work, 35
Liberals, 30, 41, 53-54, 97, 118
Libya, 141-42
Life expectancy, 8
Literacy campaign, 9, 134
Loans, 15, 48
Looting, 101, 102, 103
López, Santos, 9
López Pérez, Rigoberto, 32, 54
López Portillo, José, 49
Lumumba, Patrice, 44
Luxuries, 15

Magnavox, 24
Malaria, 25
Malnutrition, 25
Marines, 8, 27, 47, 146; and Domini-
    can Republic, 28
Martí, Farabundo, 132
Martial law, 55
Marx, Karl, 29
Marxism-Leninism, 35
Marxists, 31
Masses, 58, 59, 61, 70; and insurrec-
    tion, 62, 70; participation of, 71,
    130
Mass movement, 70, 136
Mass transit, 15
Mass work, 38
Matamoros, Lucía, 83
Maternity leave, 20
Mayorga, Silvio, 9
Medical care, 9, 10, 18
Messengers of the Word, 106
Mexico, 51
Middle class, 118, 119, 120
Middle East, 48
Military service, 22
Militia, 131

Ministry of the Interior, 88, 89
Miskitos, 19
Moncada, José Maria, 27
Monimbó uprising, 64, 65
Monroe Doctrine, 8, 26, 146
Morales, Luis, 32-33
Morales, Ricardo, 58, 81
Mugabe, Robert, 47n
Munguía, Edgar, 57
Muzorewa, Abel, 46-47, 47n

Namibia, 46
National Guard, 7, 8, 23, 87, 102-3
—abolition of, 21
—and churches, 106
—formation of, 13, 27
—hatred of, 86
—and vice, 18
Nationalizations, 9, 15, 49, 50, 96,
    120
National Palace, 66, 69
National Security Council, 7
Neighborhood committees, 62
Nicaraguan Institute of Agrarian
    Reform, 123
Nicaraguan Socialist Party, 23, 31,
    34; and class collaboration, 31, 41;
    and Somoza, 31-32
Nonaligned movement, 43, 45, 50,
    143

Oil, 25, 123, 124
Organization of American States, 49
Ortega, Camilo, 62, 63, 64
Ortega, Daniel, 43, 63, 129
Ortega, Humberto, 53

Pablo Ubeda Column, 56, 63
Palestine Liberation Organization,
    48, 142
Panama, 46
Panamerican Conference (1928), 43
Pancasán, 36, 37
Pardons. *See* Prisoners, release of
Pastora, Edén, 63, 99
Peace, 20, 151

Peace Corps, 20
Peaceful coexistence, 45
Peasants, 9, 16, 18, 36; and armed
    struggle, 22, 30, 37, 68
Pierce, Franklin, 26
Plan for Economic Reactivation, 117
Platt Amendment, 147
Pluralism, 95, 96, 97, 133
Police, 88
Polisario Front, 46, 142
Politicians, 19
Pomares, Germán, 63, 69, 71, 135
Population, 48, 114
Pornography, 98, 100
Poverty, 144
Priests, 20, 108, 109
Prisoners, 19, 87, 90, 92; release of,
    93, 98
Prisons, 90, 91-92
Privileges, 139
Proletarian Tendency, 81
Proletariat. *See* Workers
Prolonged People's War Tendency, 81
Prostitution, 18, 19-20
Public employees, 137
Puerto Rico, 46, 142, 147

Radio Corporacíon, 97, 98
Radio Sandino, 66, 76, 77, 98
Rasiratekat, Didier, 51
Raudeles, Ramón, 32, 54
Reagan, Ronald, 143
Rear guard, 78
Reconstruction, 120, 133
Religion, 105-111
Religious beliefs, 20
Repression, 56, 70, 86; against
    guerrillas, 54, 61; in cities, 55, 57
Republican Mobilization Group, 35
Revolution: causes of, 144, 146; char-
    acter of, 103; support for, 94-95
Revolutionary consciousness, 37
Revolutionary Democratic Front, 152
Revolutionary government, 14, 95.
    See also Government of National
    Reconstruction

Revolutionary war. *See* Armed struggle
Reyes, Heriberto, 32-33
Rivero, Filemón, 57
Roosevelt, Franklin D., 8
Roosevelt, Theodore, 148
Ruiz, Henry, 132

Sacasa, Juan B., 30
Saccio Vásquez Carrizosa Treaty, 149
SALT II, 49
Sandinista Defense Committees, 50
Sandinista National Liberation Front, 7, 35, 58, 68, 90, 94
—authority of, 40, 54
—formation of, 9, 13, 34, 54, 128, 129
—and Nicaraguan Socialist Party, 34
—offensive of, 55, 57, 60
—split in, 80-81, 81-82
—unity of, 69, 77, 83
Sandinista People's Army, 50, 53
Sandino, Augusto César, 8, 27, 41, 47, 53, 128; and Panamerican Conference, 43
Schick, René, 28, 34
Scholarships, 16
Sectarianism, 38
Services, growth of, 121, 122
Simón Bolivar Brigade, 101
Sixth Summit. *See* Nonaligned movement
Slavery, 26, 45, 147
Smuggling, 19
Socialist Party. *See* Nicaraguan Socialist Party
Socialist revolution, 40
Social security, 17, 18
Solidarity, 21, 79-80, 113, 125
Somoza, Anastasio, 7, 57, 64, 67, 85-86; expropriations of, 9, 14-15; overthrow of, 53, 76-77; and Vietnam, 28; wealth of, 8, 24
Somoza García Anastasio, 8, 13, 23, 28, 47; assassination of, 32, 54; coup of, 30; and Nicaraguan Socialist Party, 32

Somozaists, 7, 50, 149
South Africa, 141-42
South West Africa People's Organisation, 46, 142
Soviet Union, 147
Spain, 26, 29
Special Tribunals, 93, 99-100
Split, 80-81, 81-82
Sports, 18
State of Siege, 55
State Security, 88, 89
Stimson, Henry L., 27
Student movement, 35
Students, 16, 17
Sugar, 24
Sumos, 19

Taxes, 15, 18-19, 120
Teachers, 16-17
Television, 98
Téllez, Dora, 83
Third World, 45, 115, 124; economic crisis in, 143, 144
Tipitapa prison, 92
Tirado, Victor, 63
Tobacco, 116
Torrijos, Omar, 49
Torture, 85, 86, 88
Trade unions, 56, 61
Tuberculosis, 25
Turcios, Oscar, 58, 80

Uganda, 45
Underdevelopment, 115
Underground activity, 34. *See also* Armed struggle
Unemployment, 18
Ungo, Guillermo, 151
United People's Movement, 62
United States, 7, 8, 10, 13, 23, 24; aggression of, 26-29, 46, 47, 146-49; aid from, 50, 125; Blacks in, 21; foreign policy of, 56-57
Unity, 41, 69, 77, 83; national, 117, 119, 120
University reform, 16, 17

Uprisings, 73; at Monimbó, 64, 65; of 1977, 66, 68-69
Urban reform, 18
Urban resistance, 38, 39-40
Usury, 15

Vacations, 18
Vanderbilt, Cornelius, 26
Van Troi, Nguyen, 44
Vice industry, 18
Vietnam, 28, 41, 46, 142

Walker, William, 26, 45, 147
War, 51, 131, 151
Weapons, 67, 68, 74, 76, 77, 131
Western Sahara, 46
Wheelock, Jaime, 113, 131

Women, 20-21, 83-84
Worker-Peasant alliance, 13
Workers, 15, 18, 30, 114, 121
—and armed struggle, 22, 38
—demands of, 133
—and revolution, 130, 133, 136
—rights of, 9, 14, 17-18
—in U.S., 10
Workers' control, 9-10, 15
Workers' movement, 31, 32
World War II, 30, 31

Zambia, 141-42
Zambos, 19
Zeledón, Benjamín, 27, 147
Zimbabwe, 46-47, 141-42